a year on facebook

peter carlaftes

THREE ROOMS PRESS

New York

A Year on Facebook

Cover Illustrations:
Laurence Groux (laurencegroux.com)

Cover and Interior Design:
Kat Georges Design, New York (katgeorges.com)

Research Engineer: Max Carlaftes

First Edition

Printed in the United States of America

ISBN: 978-0-9840700-3-9

LIBRARY OF CONGRESS CATALOGING-IN-PUBLICATION DATA
Carlaftes, Peter
A Year on Facebook / Peter Carlaftes.
p. cm.
ISBN: 978-0-9840700-3-9
1. Carlaftes, Peter 2. Humor—General 3. Computers—Web—Social Networking 4. Social Science—Popular Culture—General I. Title.
Numerical coding pending.

Printed in the United States of America

Text set in Helvetica Neue 11.75/18

Published by Three Rooms Press, New York

www.threeroomspress.com
www.myspace.com/threeroomspressms
facebook group: Three Rooms Press

info@threeroomspress.com

the
book is
dedicated to
all preferences

[INTRO]

[TO THE INTRO]

I first Googled my name in 2002. There were—oh, maybe, about a couple of hundred entries, mostly from productions of plays I'd put up at the theater I co-ran in the 90s.

I especially liked seeing the review of my play *Anity*, which began with the sentence "Peter Carlaftes is Crazy." But how long could I expect that sentence to keep a smile on my face? Not long—let me tell you . . . On to next.

Next, came the stroke of brilliance: "*Where* to submit my play *Anity*." So . . . I typed in the words "Play" and "Submission" and five years later (see "porn website"), the world and I were ready for Social Networking.

PART ONE

[PRE-RAMBLE]

Social Networking, hmmm . . . I want to be seen and heard . . . Who doesn't—Right? . . .

(Somewhere Mid-2007 on a website one click away)

Let's take a look-see . . . uhhhhh, MySpace? No . . . MySpace doesn't cut it . . . (for me). I felt old(er). All the bands sounded like the days we used to sing into lightbulbs to Vanilla Fudge bashing out "You Keep Me Hanging On" . . . only—now, they all had state of the art equipment . . . and—most of them—very little else . . .

Ahhh, but what the hell? . . . There's 14 billion other pages of people with dreams—what's this? *Hamlet For Dyslexics* . . . hmmm . . . *"Be to not or be to . . . question the is that?"* Jeez . . . The victim-friendly have inherited the virtual earth . . . Well, there are people on here that I do know. Wait! Who's Tom? Silly looking kid. Bad complexion. What's that? He's got to be my friend . . . Why come? Oh, I get it . . . Pretty sneaky.

Little Brother is watching. They switched it around. Who's *They*? The powers that be and record every nano it takes for each to change a preference and figure out why. *Them, They, Those.* Who.

How could I ever go up against these cold hard facts and distinguish myself? Well, at first, I lied—but . . . my heart really wasn't in the lie. Anyone could lie, right? *I am 24 years of age. I am born under the sign of Cancer. I was born on the stairs of the Eiffel Tower . . . My, aren't you fortunate! . . . Why? . . . To have lived through such an ordeal . . . Oh . . .*

Sympathy abounds. There is no possible way to rise above the rabble. An acquired list of all who've accepted these lies is all my page will ever be . . . seems worse than a slab at the morgue. Jeez—and this is still my choice, right?

Nix Myspace. Uh, Wait! What's this?

It's a video of four young starlets, standing in a circle tonguing each other, called *I'd Like to Buy a Vowel*, and now they've stopped tonguing just long enough for each to shoot back a shot of something orange and now one runs offscreen—probably to projectile vomit—while the other three resume licking the other two's tongues . . . hmmm, probably better off with the porn—No!

It's Moving-Forward Time, although—thinking back on the sweet bird of youth and trying to get in the wagon—then, when the girl said that she had a headache—well, more often than not—this meant something else. But, now . . . their headaches must be frighteningly real after downing 50 shots of sweetened Stoli/Orangina.

My Social Networking wasn't (hardly). What else was I to do besides come to terms with the fact that—all, one day—will fall apart while holding some derivative of Oprah Winfrey's hand.

PART TWO

[SPONTANEOUS INDUCTION]

080808

Peter Carlaftes is creating . . .

20 seconds ago · Comment

"Is Creating" was my first Status Update, when I joined Facebook on 08/08/08. And I was creating: A Being . . . a Presence.

Where were you on 08/08/08?

On 06/06/06, I was eagerly waiting outside Notre Dame Cathedral, just in case those crazy gargoyles suddenly sprang to life . . . but—nothing (good or evil) made them do it, so here—(on 08/08/08)—Facebook seemed a more likely surface for a weed like me to push through a crack and create something new.

Call it a hunch. I took it on . . . supplied the correct information and presto . . . Peter Carlaftes (the profile) was born.

Sex: (no funny answers) *Male* . . . **Hometown:** *the city that never sleeps* . . . I look out my window at the never ending parade of these newfound ageless frat boys and valley girls—who all act like they're treading on each others' movie set; some fight, some fall in love; none are more than a heel click away from some bff's wedding in Vegas (then what?) . . . *New York, New York.*

Relationship Status: (ahhh, just leave it) *Single* (for now) . . .

Looking For: (well—um, what are my choices?)—*Friendship* —(Boom) and just like that, I had my first friend —who welcomed me into the vortex to be. Then, soon after changing my **Relationship Status**, my new friend quickly wrote back: So—now—You're *Married?*

Whereby, I tacked on *Networking* to **Looking For** right below *Friendship* . . . which gave me an idea . . .

PART THREE

[A FACEBOOK-WORM TURNS]

What was my idea? Well, my wishful-thinking motive for joining Facebook was actually This: I was performing a one-man show *Lenny Bruce: Dead and Well*—wherein Beat Comic Lenny Bruce comes back to Earth with new irreverent takes, and I saw that the Lenny Bruce Facebook fanbase was ripe for solicitation. So, I built the rest of my profile on that basis (attracting the Lenny Bruce fan) to possibly put a few more butts in the seats, adding the deceptively truthful tidings:

Political Views:	Everyone tries to get what they want
Religious Views:	Everyone dies trying

I also posted videos of the Lenny show from Youtube on my page, which apparently did the trick because I soon had hundreds of friends . . .

INTERACTIVE ALERT

This is link to one of the Lenny show videos. You the reader, can cut this link out of the book and paste it (literally) right to your computer screen on the browser of your choice. If it works, let me know and we'll get a team together to approach the big boys.

Next, came forming the group for Three Rooms Press—which meant asking those of a poetical, literary or theatrical bent to join. I befriended the author, the lit mag, the playwright, the agent, etc.—anyone that might help professionally. Some smart aleck suggested a psychiatrist.

Then, I befriended anyone with a famous last name: the Churchill, the Barrymore, the Ellington, etc.—just in case they might be related (and could help with money they inherited).

I soon had thousands of friends.

Having moved around so much as a kid, an acquaintance suggested my quest to have so many Facebook friends was a way to make up for years of lost youth—and, be that as it may—the search went on and on and on.

Awaiting friend confirmation

PART FOUR

[MAN-INFEST JESTINY]

While padding friends, I found the odds were:

6 out of 10 ignored my request

3 out of 10 accepted my request, and

1 out of 10 always wrote the same message,

"How do I know you?"

to which I always answered, *"Perhaps you saw the* America's Most Wanted *episode about the kid who killed everyone in his small town when he was 13 and just escaped from the maximum security psychiatric ward?"*

None out of any 10 ever replied.

Then, being a film buff, I joined many groups and pages for actors, directors and movies, and doing so inspired me (also being a lover of wordplay and puns) to create my own group: Angels With Dirty Facebook . . .

> **Description:** juvenile delinquents who have come of age and straightened out due to every facet of facebook . . .
>
> please choose your favorite dead end kid, and—whomever gets the most votes is the leader of the gang . . . and—whomever finds out if whomever is grammatically correct (in this instance) gets a two-thirds cut in the next job . . .

And, then—through my status updates—the irreverent observation became an identity . . . the pun—a place to be.

So these are all my updates deemed worthy to inspire, including the responses from all my many friends, as well as little blurbs from yours truly on the side.

And, one more thing—

> **@%#&@!!! We have to go to press now!**
> **There isn't time for one more thing!!**
>
> ***—Editor***

—Just one more thing:

Being Cyberspace-Crafted, this book is designed to be interactive with its sister website: www.ayearonfacebook.com.

So . . .

Enjoy and Be Inspired.

—P.C.

[INTER-ACTIVE-MEZZO]

Log in and find out how to watch me and my computer image alternate reading this intro to each other on your very own computer at:

www.ayearonfacebook.com

[START]

UPDATES and RESPONSE

081508

Peter Carlaftes hello all my new facebook friends and all of your facebook friends . . . i thought my razor was dull until i heard this speech. Which reminds me of a story so dirty i'm ashamed to even think of it myself . . .

What better way to start than steal from Groucho?

been working on channeling my lenny bruce bit. videos are posted on youtube with more lenny. just put my name plus his together and boom—like magic—the 21st century is yours.

also check out *The Cut-Off Point,* a short we did along the lorena bobbitt lines (but without the husbands penis)—you'll have to see for yourselves . . .

Hey, you too can check it out on youtube.

happy to be aboard . . .

081708

Peter Carlaftes we all know what happened to the last one who kept himself surrounded by a sea of friends . . .

Et tu, Bruté . . .

081808

Peter Carlaftes and don't forget the other one that surrounded himself w/friends for dinner—boom . . .

Betrayed . . .
I N R E . . .

082408

Peter Carlaftes has nothing to hide (under) . . .

YOUR PHOTO HERE

Comment

Remember when authoritarian figures told you not to write it that book—well, that was then—and this book has been formatted for the reader to also write in, that is—unless it's not your book . . . so, if this book isn't yours, go out and buy one of your own and read and write to your heart's content . . .

—Author

Are you completely out of your mind?

—Editor

091008

Peter Carlaftes went from not being to Provence . . .

Actually took a little jaunt to Provence—which helped inspire this book (see *A Year In Provence*) but—while there—there went Lehman Brothers . . .

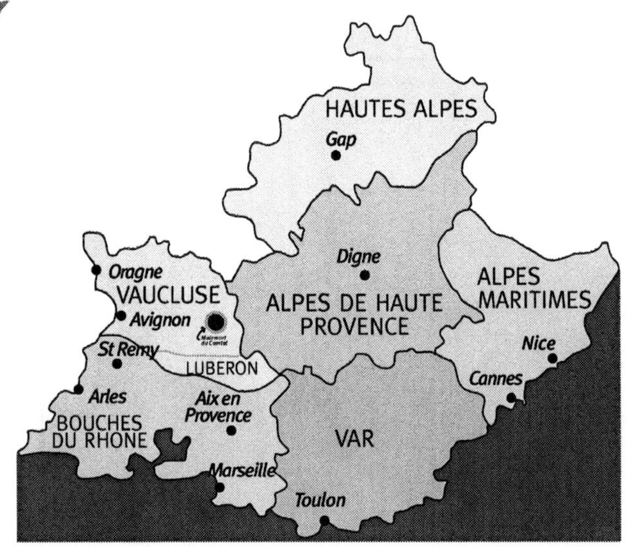

092708

Peter Carlaftes can eat 50 eggs . . .

Homage to Paul Newman's passing . . .

> **a.k.** nobody can eat 50 eggs.
>
> **t.c.** If my boy says he can eat 50 eggs in an hour, by God, he can eat 50 eggs in an hour.
>
> **a.s.** What we've got here is failure to communicate!!

102008

Peter Carlaftes is all the page . . .

> **s.g.** somebody's having a punny day.
>
> **p.c.** think i could give you a pun for your money?

Took a little time to get rolling . . .

110408

Peter Carlaftes is glad to share the joy of seeing so much sadness from the past melt away . . .

> **f.c.** So beautifully put. Thanks . . .
>
> **a.r.** This is the greatest night I've ever lived
>
> **j.c.** have to agree that's a very eloquent way of summing up the joy I think many people from all backgrounds are feeling right now.

Election night 2008!

111308

Peter Carlaftes says today's the day that Felix Unger's wife threw him out . . .

For *Odd Couple* fans . . .

r.n. Deep down, he knew she was right, but he also knew that someday, he would return to her.

j.p. We're all out of cornflakes. F.U.

s.g. "Don't assume, because when you assume you make and Ass out of U and Me."

s.b. When I told some of the kids at work that today was Felix Unger Day so many had no idea what I was talking about. Thanks for being old enough to know.

k.g. Raise a (carefully sterilized) glass to Felix's health!

111508

Peter Carlaftes wants to open a restaurant called Hardy Tartare . . .

The start of starting a punny business series . . .

> **r.n.** Man, that's got me Lulzin over here.
>
> **a.a.** hehe
>
> **s.h.** I like that name.
>
> **p.c.** I like yours, too . . .
>
> **l.l.** I have the great desire to open an Indian consignment shop called "Who's Sari Now"

111608

Peter Carlaftes wants to open an employment agency called
Ready! Lame! Fired! . . .

> **a.m.** Ha! Wish I was back in NYC to see you in action.
>
> **l.p.** You are the King of Puns!
>
> **m.h.** wants to open a law firm called Dewey, Cheatum and Howe. Hang on that was Leisure Suit Larry.

111708

Peter Carlaftes wants to open a hat shop (millinery) called Hip-Hip Beret . . .

> **l.p.** I'd shop there. ;)

111808

Peter Carlaftes is going to work out at Jehovah's Fitness . . .

> **d.m.** haha!
>
> **f.f.** DOG bless you
>
> **n.s.** Cool—Jehovah and Out Peter—see you in Kingdom Hall! ;-)
>
> **d.e.** Spiritual Aerobics—Stand Up, Reach Out, Pull In, Kneel, Lift Up!

111908

Peter Carlaftes wants to open a bagel shop called Fort Lox . . .

> **h.h.** Sorry there is 1 in NY state.
>
> **j.r.** but not nyc!
>
> **b.c.** anything to go would be fort lox in a box, and that's without even beginning to work with dr suess rhymes . . .
>
> **p.p.** MMMmm . . . Can you do a delivery service to the UK?
>
> **a.h.** Done.
>
> **s.m.** Whatever, just call yours "Better than Fort Lox."
>
> **w.a.** Lox, stocks and two smoking bagels.
>
> **s.m.** alright alright then, no racket in the back room, no mysterious customers, no topless ladies rollin dough, no fun.
>
> **s.c.** I LOVE THIS! :)

112008

Peter Carlaftes wants to start a children's clothing line called Oscar de Placenta . . .

> **s.j.** Next door to Gucci Gucci-Coo?
>
> **s.t.** LOL. Very funny!
>
> **p.c.** this line is for infants and you take a sonogram of the fetus before birth which takes all the proper measurements so the baby will feel as one with the material world when it is born into fitted clothes, a take somewhat on the leboyer method with water—one might think . . .
>
> **a.m.** you're killing me with this pun fest.
>
> **l.w.** keep em up!
>
> **m.p.** And one of yr designers is Vera Waaaahhhh-Ng . . . ?

112108

Peter Carlaftes wants to open a landscape service called Avant Yard . . .

> **r.m.** hehe. it's a little funny.

112208

Peter Carlaftes wants to film a video of the Vegan Work It Out . . .

Beatles fans revolt . . . (by omission)

Peter Carlaftes wants to film a video of *The Out of Workout* . . .

> **j.k.** You should write a book—these are better than sniglets.
>
> **p.c.** ok—that'll be 20 bucks for the reading . . .
>
> **s.g.** Proprietor: Crystal Ball?

What's a "sniglet"?

A sniglet is "any word that doesn't appear in the dictionary, but should."

—*Editor*

112308

Peter Carlaftes has a-Hemming-way with Words . . .

> **d.w.** You yell while you get drunk and beat your wife?
>
> **c.c.** the importance of being ernest ? lol
>
> **d.o.** "We are all apprentices in a craft where no one ever becomes a master . . . "
>
> **j.r.** dude, a pun a day keeps the ________ away . . .

112408

Peter Carlaftes wants to start a children's dentistry outfit called Babe Tooth . . .

> **m.s.** You're Jawsome!
>
> **d.g.** you can't handle the tooth.
>
> **b.s.** I always wanted to develop a snack product for literary types called DerridOs.
>
> **p.c.** I have Ego Chips . . . when you're not full enough of yourself . . .

112508

Peter Carlaftes wants to start an orthodontics outfit called Teenage Braceland . . .

> **s.a.** Ha!
>
> **m.h.** you've heard of dreaming in another language? Last night I had a dream segment composed entirely in Peter Carlaftes puns.
>
> **n.d.** What about a window replacement outfit called King of Pane? Or, better yet, an online typeface store called Eminence Font? A US-based analytical society called Jung Americans? A cellular phone aimed at young women called Girls Just Want to Have Phone?

112608

Peter Carlaftes is getting (excitedly) ready to watch *Judge Nudie* . . .

> **r.c.** As long as you don't nudge Judy with a rudie.

If you, the reader, turn this book sideways now—and shake it from side to side—you, the reader, will hear the sound of a martini being shaken and, if this doesn't work for some odd reason, you, the reader, can click on the cocktail shaker icon at ayearonfacebook.com

112708

Peter Carlaftes was just hit by a car on the Hit By a Car Facebook Application, which doesn't exist as this doesn't really exist, now—does it?

> **s.t.** Some of these applications are a pain in the butt.
>
> **s.b.** Some? Shall we go for almost all.
>
> **t.s.** Maybe Harvey was behind the wheel . . .
>
> **p.c.** me and Harvey, we go to the bars and we listen to all the horrible bad things that people have done and all the great wonderful things they're going to do . . . because no one brings anything small into a bar . . .
>
> **d.m.** I like that !
>
> **s.b.** You can always count on a six foot tall rabbit to offer wisdom.

112808

Peter Carlaftes wants to start a kosher line of holiday spirits called Synagrog . . .

> **e.s.** The unappetizing, yet ecumenical, dairy line is Syneggnog
>
> **p.c.** we'll passover that remark . . .

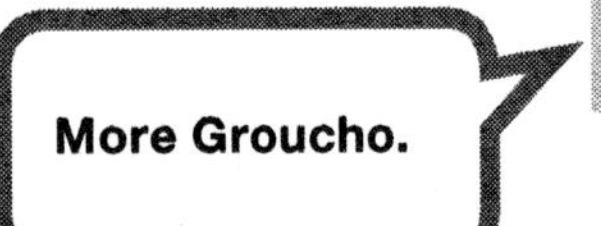

113008

Peter Carlaftes is going to listen to the Tuning Forchestra . . .

> **w.a.** Is it the Last Night of the Prongs?
>
> **p.c.** it's a virtue-so-so . . .

Wouldn't it be cool to have a whole stage of tuning forks?

Very heavy metal.

—Editor

120108

Peter Carlaftes is reading the exploits of blind criminal Felon Keller . . .

> **a.k.** catskills look out!

Peter Carlaftes is going to listen to the Forgiven Quartet perform the *Death-Warmed Over-ture* . . .

> **One word: Forget . . .**
>
> ***—Editor***

120208

Peter Carlaftes sadly just bet on a horse called: But Not Least . . .

> **b.b.** . . . so, good luck !!!! And . . . I bet on it too !!!!!

Peter Carlaftes is writing a new hit song for the times, *Take This Job And Covet* . . .

> **k.g.** you're killin me.
>
> **d.r.** Lol . . . Sign of the times.
>
> **r.m.** I'm seriously considering unfriending you.
>
> **p.c.** please don't . . . i'm manic possessive . . .
>
> **r.m.** that was funny enough that i'll hold off for a bit

r.m. unfriended me shortly thereafter.

unfriend |ˌən-ˈfrend | **1.** To remove someone from your Livejournal, MySpace, Facebook, or other social networking site. Doing this is often seen as a passive-aggressive move, telling the person without telling them that you no longer want to be friends. It's also commonly a response to drama. Unfriending someone often causes more drama. There are sometimes valid reasons for doing this.

120308

Peter Carlaftes new excuse for being late for work is oversleptical . . .

Should've been a "sleeper" . . . hahaha . . .

> **j.r.** that's a keeper!
>
> **l.m.** At the very least I smile every time.
>
> **s.g.** me too! i would comment more often if it weren't for all these damn papers i have to grade . . .

Peter Carlaftes has a degree in malarcheology . . .

Yeah, a Third Degree Borscht Belt . . .

Peter Carlaftes will get it done, even if it takes Inactive God . . .

> **j.k.** Doesn't this hurt your head?
>
> **p.c.** not if it doesn't hurt yours . . .
>
> **j.k.** it doesn't but this does.
>
> **h.i.** do you have magic powers? how do you do that?
>
> **j.k.** I have no idea what you're talking about*

* http://www.revfad.com/flip.html

Peter Carlaftes wants to start a computer dating service called E42 . . .

> **j.m.** that's a good Idea i hope it works.
>
> **r.c.** Well that sounds better than 24T.
>
> **n.d.** Hey, Would you like to help me write a nonfiction book about the federal bailout of the auto industry? It's called THE LAST TEMPTATION OF CHRYSLER.
>
> **p.c.** i think i'd be ford out of my mind . . .

This one was better than the status (by far)

Peter Carlaftes has a new sign on the door to his facebook page: Beware of Dog-geral . . .

> **c.f.** I once considered launching an urban magazine for dogs called HEREBOI.

Both have fleas . . .

—Editor

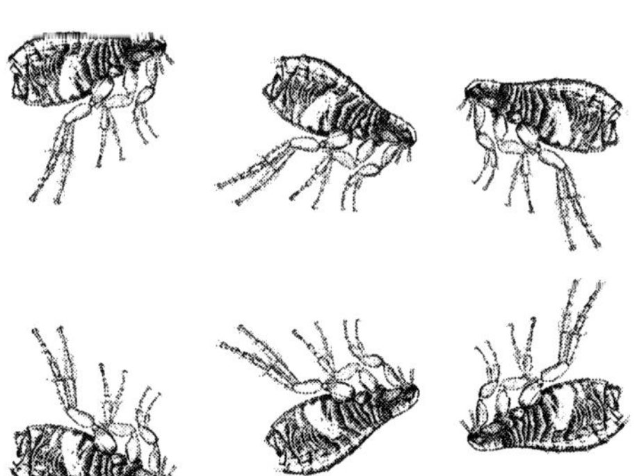

120408

Peter Carlaftes is sorry he brought the kids to Judgment Daycare . . .

> **p.r.** OK that sounds like a good story there . . . do tell.
>
> **p.c.** can't . . . the world ended . . .

Peter Carlaftes just bought tickets for a cruise from Tour de Norse to somewhere out of the Fjordinary . . .

Arguably: the worst update. . .

No argument.

—Editor

Peter Carlaftes just bought a cold sore medicine called Cancres Away . . .

> **j.m.** you may need to take zinc & Vit C to boost your immunity.
>
> **s.c.** The best cold sore medicine I ever used is called Abreva
>
> **p.c.** this stuff doesn't work . . .
> now i'm going to try Herpes Herpes Cheap Cheap . . .

Peter Carlaftes is ready for some Spanish Foreplay: Por Favorgasm . . .

> **f.h.** Ok. It's a great daily (or hourly) pleasure. I'm loving it. But this time you pushed it too far.
>
> **p.c.** you're lucky i left off Either/Orifice . . .

Peter Carlaftes just bought identical twin beds . . .

Guess I was two sheets to the wind . . .

> **t.s.** You keep me laughing. Thanks for sitting on my facebook . . .
>
> **s.z.** " . . . but forgot to buy the twins"

Peter Carlaftes has decided to buy a shrubbery at Jules Fern . . .

> **p.p.** Bring us a shrubbery.
>
> **s.t.** Are you getting a Bush?
>
> **k.g.** I'd prefer a herring . . .
>
> **t.c.** I went there to get the garden pond fronds package, 20,000 Leaves Under the Sea.

Upsetting when responses are wittier . . .

120508

Peter Carlaftes is going to whip his work history into shape using Resumatrix . . .

> **s.s.** Won't you be using "a" Resumatrix? What are they charging these days?
>
> **p.c.** it's a fictional software package that allows one to make a super resume and have fun doing it and, even though this doesn't exist—someone has the domain name so power to them . . . but, most of all, power to the imagination . . .

120608

Peter Carlaftes is reading
Cannery Row'Connor . . .

> **a.h.** She's my absolute favorite. I'm writing a paper on her exactly now.
>
> **p.c.** hey watch out . . . the life you save may be your own (or at least second-mortgaged) from a good man that isn't very hard to find . . .
>
> **a.h.** I'm constantly reminding these displaced persons up in here that everything that rises must converge, like geraniums in the river. If you have wise blood, you'll understand why the violent bear it away. Sexuality is violence and violence is Grace.

120708

Peter Carlaftes is reading a bio of Siegfried and Roy called *Tamer vs. Tamer* . . .

> **j.r.** i can't stop giggling.
>
> **s.b.** No way . . . That's hilarious! :-D
>
> **a.m.** HA!
>
> **j.p.** :D
>
> **p.c.** someone has asked me why this is funny and i'm trying to think of what to tell them . . .
>
> **s.b.** If they are very, very young . . . you might have to explain the whole *Kramer vs Kramer* thing :-)
>
> **p.c.** that's exactly what i did . . .
>
> **g.d.** the tiger in question released a recipe book just in time for xmas
>
> **p.c.** the book in question will be titled *What to Do with Corduroy* (quarter roy) . . .

120808

Peter Carlaftes just bought a new CD called *Hooked On King* . . . (Ben E., B.B., Carol, etc)

Other ideas start flowing . . .

> **r.c.** I would buy a spoken word CD called Hooked on Simpson . . . with famous sound bites from Jessica, O.J., Homer, etc.
>
> **p.c.** *Hooked on Sting*?
>
> **m.p.** Bees, hornets, wasps, etc . . . ?
>
> **c.c.** i just bought a cd of george bush's famous speeches . . . the cd was blank! hehehehe :-)

Peter Carlaftes wants to create a new reality show: *One Night Standid Camera* . . .

> **j.c.** I wanna be on the show. Ted Turner will see it, and buy us both a ranch in Montana.
>
> **p.c.** hey, let's grow some dental floss . . .
>
> **g.d.** i was thinking the other day about a reality show set in an intensive care unit. every week, we get to know more about the patients and then vote to see who gets their life support machines switched off!
>
> **p.c.** let's call it Plug of War . . .

Peter Carlaftes wants to shoot a new version of *Ben Hur-bie* . . . (chariot race with the love bug) . . .

> **s.c.** alright . . . that's funny! :)
>
> **p.c.** once in a while—there's magic . . .
>
> **s.c.** I'm trying to envision Heston in a bug, lol!
>
> **m.w.** hahaha!! That's the best one yet! :-))

120909

Peter Carlaftes wants a kinder, gentler weapon which blows up the target but also feeds the survivors called the Cous-Cruise Missile . . .

> **c.c.** the cous cous can also accompany the coup coup missile. mass populated intergrated flavour!
>
> **k.c.** They may need to make a diet version in case the targets are a group of tween fashion models/actresses with body image issues. They could call it the 100 calorie Olson Twinkie.
>
> **c.c.** the 100 calorie praying mantis diet lol.
>
> **k.c.** hah much better!

. . . Others start communicating . . .

121008

Peter Carlaftes is watching the Disney classic about the alcoholic scientist called *Honey, I Drank the Kids* . . .

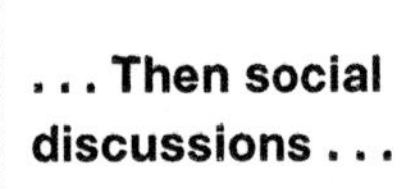

w.a. I've met him. The kids went down the drain, but he has 12 years sober.

a.s. lol well at least he's sober

p.c. he downed his oldest kid as a flaming shot . . . hey! why does he have to be a he —like . . . why can't a woman be a scientist or at least an alcoholic . . .

w.a. He is a she now. An unexpected gift of sobriety.

p.c. maybe she could wear Tranves-Tights . . . the latest rage in shemale clothing . . . hides your you-know-whatee . . .

a.s. wait what, he's a she? o goodness gracious . . . send links!

k.c. it doesn't matter if it's a he or a she . . . as long as you get paid.

b.f. Amazing idea.

Peter Carlaftes is watching a new show on the Discovery Channel called *Jacques Cousteau-Away* . . .

. . . And, then—sadly—this one . . .

—Editor

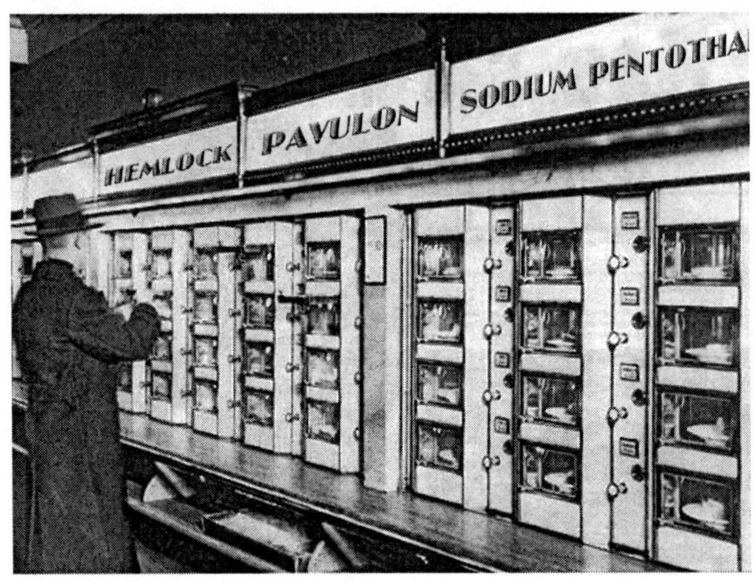

121108

Peter Carlaftes says for legally assisted suicide you can plead Self Dispense . . .

> **k.e.** ohhhhh . . .
>
> **g.d.** it's civic duty! save taxpayer money!!!
>
> **s.g.** awesome.
>
> **e.d.** what exquisitely shameless punnery, sir.

Peter Carlaftes wants to open a tattoo removal parlor called Scar Wash . . .

> **j.v.** YES WEEK-END !!!!
>
> **c.n.** Will you expand to stretch lines and facial surgery remnants?
>
> **p.c.** anything for a tuck (i mean buck) . . .
>
> **m.b.** Sign me up . . .
>
> **j.c.** They'll never take my tattoos!!
>
> **s.m.** This gal loves scars and tats—so the "Scar Wash" ain't for me

Peter Carlaftes says, How about giving Caroline Kennedy Obama's seat?

> **f.f.** back in 2001 i finally met her. on the 79th street crosstown bus.
>
> **p.p.** are you saying that "you" gave her "your" seat?
>
> **g.d.** what's Obama supposed to sit on?

121209

Peter Carlaftes will trade Hillary's Seat for one Springsteen Super Bowl Halftime Show . . .

> **a.g.** good idea. even if Springsteen is not one my of favourites, it will be better than Hillary's seat
>
> **j.w.** I always thought Bruce Springsteen had a nicer seat than Hillary Clinton.
>
> **a.l.** I'm thinking he will include: "Born to Run," possibly "Hungry Heart," "Glory Days," possibly "I'm on Fire," "Born in the USA," and one of the new ones like "Radio Nowhere!" Oh yeah! He has to come on stage in one of those Rocket Packs Michael Jackson used 20 years ago!!!
>
> **p.c.** he'll be changing the song titles to "Worn to Run" for Nike and "Glory Pays" for the Army . . .
>
> **m.p.** Mebbe you'd get a two-fer . . . Hillary's got some ample pants suited *seat* there . . . not that I'm checking out her ass or anything. I'm just glad she's not gonna be my NY state junior senatress no more . . . oh, wait, yeah, but . . . now she's ALL our Sec o'State . . . nevermind.

Peter Carlaftes suffers from Self-Centerprise . . .

> **l.d.** ha! There's a lot of that going around . . . ;)
>
> **a.h.** oh yes, I remember that—with its crew's five year mission to make things nice for themselves; "stuff the federation of planets," said the crew of starship Self-Centerprise, "it's all too much like hard work dealing with people, let alone alien races . . . " The remains of the crew were last heard of living on 42 different planets, studiously ignoring each other and dying out one by one . . .
>
> **m.m.** *hands a.h. a gold star for his efforts*
>
> **p.c.** why—it's a great american tradition.
>
> **m.m.** I'm sorry, I did not hear you. I was thinking about myself.
>
> **m.b.** yeap . . . it is an american tradition

And here—even whole scenarios!

121308

Peter Carlaftes is trying his darndest to read poems by Robert in Japanese called *Frost in Translation* . . .

> **j.h.** しかし私は私が眠る前に保つ 約束および行くマイルを有する
>
> **d.o.** here is what happens when put Frost through a Japanese translator and back into English: It could curve 2 these roads with the yellow wood, And it could not travel regrettable me both And length 1 travelers stood me, be And I was possible, if with being seen under one, did that with the grass bend somewhere?; Then fair other things were taken exactly, And a perhaps it has better request, Because that the grass grew thick, was the wear which was desired; But in regard to that cross there Those of the almost same rank were attached to the body really And you put in place both that morning equally Step did not step on black with the leaf. Well, I maintained between 1st of another day! However method how brings method, you have known,

If I returned me, it doubted. I say sigh remain It ages somewhere, therefore ages: Wood and I-[de] it could curve 2 these roads I took one where the travelers are few, And that caused all differences.

j.l. Might be Haiku-ish—Whose woods Are these I think I know (blablabla)

p.c. perhaps he would get kudos from his dentist (Robert Flossed) . . .

j.l. Ha! Robert Flossed . . . The ironic thing is that the austere beauty of Frost's language would probably translate better than most . . .

121408

Peter Carlaftes just heard the hippest Spanish Tribute band: The Llamas and the Tapas . . .

> **l.m.** Oh my God . . .

121508

Peter Carlaftes is listening to French Tribute band: deGaulle and Oates . . .

> **g.d.** then there's chirac a khan
>
> **a.g.** I prefer Le DeJourney or SarkoZZTop
>
> **p.c.** don't forget Bastilley Dan . . .

Quickly, lose that number . . .

—Editor

121608

Peter Carlaftes defines somebody watching a one-sided boxing match as: KO Spectate . . .

> **t.c.** Would that make the defeated boxer who never should have been there beaten to KO Jelly?
>
> **p.c.** TKY Jelly . . . cause now, they're totally screwed . . .

Peter Carlaftes would like his back pay in advance . . .

> **g.d.** that's hilarious!
>
> **p.c.** there's also the Back Down Payment . . .

Peter Carlaftes would love to crawl into a Self-RepRoach Motel . . .

> **g.d.** sir, you are, indeed, a god among men. that would make an awesome band name.

121708

Peter Carlaftes is having a banana "split" at San Andreas Malt . . .

> **j.w.** It beats a banana "spit."
>
> **j.r.** tee hee. hee!

121808

Peter Carlaftes needs an Attorney-In-Law . . .

121908

Peter Carlaftes has one for bebop fans; visit Dizzy Gillespie's beer joint called: A-Micro-Brewnisia . . .

> **t.s.** Apparently Dizzy wasn't the only one with range! Wow . . .
>
> **s.b.** Best of the recent ones. Well done.

122008

Peter Carlaftes understands it's a point of no concern . . .

122108

Peter Carlaftes has developed an antidote to the lingering effects of Viagra called: Sex-Lax . . .

For the consummated, not constipated . . .

> **m.s.** That's clever!
>
> **m.v.** I call it a kick-stand!

122208

Peter Carlaftes is trying out a new dance craze: the Maca-Rooney . . .

Like Mickey, I'll be paying for this in the next wife —uh, life . . .

122308

Peter Carlaftes doesn't listen to Cashier-Say . . .

> **m.h.** hah, I had to read my newspeak dictionary for that one. Hang on, I'm in George Orwell mode again . . .

122408

Peter Carlaftes wishes all a happy merry as he'll pay for it afterwards . . .

122508

Peter Carlaftes changed his last name to Bank and got 2.6 trillion dollars for Christmas —whewww!

m.w. LOL! What a clever fellow you are!

w.a. Time for a $23,000,000,000 bonus, my man. Good work!

p.n. i changed my name to gypsie and well, you can imagine what happened!

a.l. yeah! i changed my name to Ford and only got $15 billion!

p.c. a.l. is a shmuck . . .

a.l. That's what I get for buying American!

p.c. a shmuck is someone that gets out of the shower to pee . . .

a.s. nice!

123108

Peter Carlaftes is gonna party like it's two thousand and nine (very prudently) . . .

Recession (proof) . . .

010109

Peter Carlaftes's hang ain't over by a long shot . . .

> **a.p.** congrats on being well-hung.
>
> **d.r.** lol . . . good one
>
> **g.d.** dear boy, how dare you sober up enough for a hangover. tut tut. won't do at all.

010209

Peter Carlaftes is gonna condom playtex distance . . .

> **t.b.** It's too early!!! What the does this mean???
>
> **p.c.** ok . . . i'll tell . . . contem-plate-ex-istence . . .
>
> **t.b.** Damn!! Just as I thought!!! Bastard peoples!!!

010309

Peter Carlaftes would like to design a honeymoon garment called: an Opening Night-Gown . . .

> **l.g.** funny! :)
>
> **l.b.** I fear it would have a very limited market . . .
>
> **p.c.** well, then we'll have to market Virgin territory . . .

010509

Peter Carlaftes has concocted a hot new red wine called: Jala-Pinot Noir . . .

> **l.g.** are you publishing these?—I see, like, a book with one per page . . .
>
> **b.g.** Do you serve it hot?
>
> **l.g.** or made by Vikings living in Mexico and call it Val-jala-pinot. . .
>
> **p.c.** hmmph . . . maybe l.g. should write their own book . . .
>
> **l.g.** Au contraire (an airline on which you're guaranteed an argument with the flight attendant), mon frere. You're an inspiration. You're pun-acious practices have gone viral. I love them.
>
> **p.c.** thank you kindly l.g . . . I could do no better in this mere mortal shell than inspire . . .

An idea is born . . . and now, at least—you have l.g. to blame . . .

010709

Peter Carlaftes mistakenly used a plumbing service called: Calamity Drain . . .

> **s.s.** Shoulda gone with Feral Fawcett instead.

010809

Peter Carlaftes's girlfriend dumped him after buying her flowers at Bon Corsage . . .

> **s.a.** !!! Man. That's terrible.
>
> **p.c.** the pun or the outcome?

011009

Peter Carlaftes would like to create an animated series about a homeless cyborg called: Skid-Robot . . .

> **c.m.** I'd watch that! I can actually imagine that as a series-within-the-series on Futurama. That would be Bender's favorite tv program.
>
> **d.l.** how about a broadway musical about the homeless
>
> **p.c.** okay . . . we'll call it Gimme Shelter (and a Dollar) . . .
>
> **d.l.** choreography with shopping carts, the possibilities for love ballad, injustice, redemption—it has it all . . .

011109

Peter Carlaftes wants to make a movie about a 70s undercover cop who accepts favors from prostitutes called: *Slurpico* . . .

> **c.w.** Ew.
>
> **s.g.** I thought Slurpico was about an undercover cop notorious for his insulting epithets.
>
> **a.l.** wants to make a movie about a 70s undercover cop who makes wild fruit flavored drinks called 'SLURPEECOS'

011209

Peter Carlaftes wants to create an all purpose face lotion that lasts for 20 years called: Lip Tan Wrinkle . . .

The rights to this product can be bought by the first check that clears . . .

> **p.m.** How about Face-Off?
>
> **a.d.** What about Pond's Daily On?
>
> **p.m.** I stole Face-Off from Putney Swope
>
> **p.c.** t and s, baby (truth and soul) . . .
>
> **p.m.** Rockin' the boat's a drag. You gotta sink the boat!
>
> **w.g.** oil of delay
>
> **p.c.** we must collaborate . . .

011309

Peter Carlaftes wants to shop at the ceasefire sale . . .

> **f.c.** Don't we all . . .
>
> **g.d.** reminds me of that classic laurel and hardy short, "tit for tat" only not in the least bit amusing.
>
> **p.h.** you'll never get to heaven on an ak47.

Peter Carlaftes wants to start a job resource pool called: Sir Free-Lancelot . . .

> **f.h.** Excellent one. How come no one seems to notice?
>
> **p.c.** fellow manimosity . . .

011409

Peter Carlaftes says one week till D.C. don't mean Dick Cheney anymore . . .

> **w.g.** less, 6 days . . . !
>
> **b.g.** I will miss Cheney, he was a such a dick.
>
> **t.c.** May The Flying Spaghetti Monster touch our pointy little heads with his noodly appendage !
>
> **p.m.** I'll miss Cheney's sneer
>
> **c.w.** What will he do with his human-sized safe? I hope there are some intrepid cameramen filming the exit.
>
> **d.w.** What a lovely thought. We had our moment DC moment here in Australia in 2007 when John Howard lost the Election to Labor. You're welcome to keep Howard now that he's back in the US for his Freedom Medal . . . and they say Americans have no idea of irony!!
>
> **t.c.** There will be a severe worldwide champagne shortage come Tuesday night.

011509

Peter Carlaftes says it's time to be done with Terristocracy . . .

> **g.d.** the war on terror makes one helluva catchy acronymn
>
> **m.s.** twot . . . lol
>
> **b.b.** but i was just starting to enjoy the manufactured angst!

011609

Peter Carlaftes needs an anti-oppressant . . .

> **m.h.** so does half the US
>
> **d.o.** haha, I am working on an anti-omniscient, I think it's called booze

Peter Carlaftes asks if I split my time between 2 bashes Tuesday will I be called Bi-Party Son . . .

> **w.g.** . . . the audacity of trope.

011709

Peter Carlaftes is singing, *Goosey in the Sky while Climbing* . . . Picture yourself on a plane on a river . . .

Commercial plane lands on Hudson River after shredded geese clogged both engines; nobody hurt—so a little humor didn't—either (hurt). . .

k.g. Wow, man. . .

a.k. sitting in a wheelchair, climbing up the eiffel tower . . .

p.c. i am the airbus . . . goo goo ga choob . . .

w.g. touche!

011909

Peter Carlaftes says, Bye-Bye Bush . . .
Yo 'Bama!

> **g.d.** i'm reserving judgement on the Obama presidency. i won't be convinced he's the right man until i hear him say the word "nukula"
>
> **p.r.** I thought it was nookuler
>
> **s.s.** YO 'BAMA!!!!!

012109

Peter Carlaftes coins the new era—Bamelot.

> **a.c.** Yes!
>
> **b.p.** you are a scribe of our time!
>
> **p.d.** "Oh, let's not go to the White House. It is such a silly place!"
>
> **r.n.** BAMELOT
> *It's true! It's true! The Prez has made a vow.*
> *Well . . . Yes i could . . . judge what you will:*
> *The country will move forward starting now.*
> *Old laws will now be made anew here:*
> *The planet's climate must not get too hot . . .*
> *And we're respecting human rights here*
> *In Bamelot.*
> *The economy will need an overhaul*
> *And bankers can't keep everything they've got.*
> *By order, we'll all answer to the call*
> *In Bamelot.*
> *Bamelot! Bamelot!*
> *I know it sounds a bit bizarre,*
> *But in Bamelot, Bamelot*
> *That's how conditions are.*
> *The choice between our ideals and safety*
> *Is one that we won't have to make here*
> *In short, there's simply not*
> *A more progressive spot*
> *For America-remaking than here*
> *In Bamelot.*

> **d.l.** I think he should have worn tights and a cape to take the oath . . .
>
> **p.m.** sounds right to me . . .
>
> **j.c.** Perfect.

012209

Peter Carlaftes says, the "real" devil . . . wears Nada . . .

> **k.t.** nice one.
>
> **w.g.** there's a "and ______ wears dada" but i'm way too tired to be clever.
>
> **p.c.** wake up and go to sleep . . .
>
> **w.g.** exactly, hello i must be going . . . zzz
>
> **m.s.** Excellent!

012309

Peter Carlaftes has developed a new breed of drug-sniffing dogs called: Co-Canines . . .

> **e.m.** LOL
>
> **g.d.** SHA-ZING! classic gag, mate.
>
> **c.c.** is right lol

012409

Peter Carlaftes booked a cruise on a stained-glass bottom boat from Sistene Travel and is gonna lay on his back for days . . .

> **p.p.** that is so awesome.

012509

Peter Carlaftes has designed a new, Battleship-type board game called: Miniature Gulf . . .

012609

Peter Carlaftes will not buy a new soft drink called: AyaCola . . .

> **m.p.** AyaCola CokeMani?
>
> **g.d.** "ayatola don't khomeini closer"
>
> **s.g.** i don't know who you are but i totally just LOLed

012709

Peter Carlaftes is after the world's oldest possession . . .

> **d.r.** That seems like an admirable profession. Does it have a uniform?
>
> **s.m.** I'm pretty sure the uniform involves hot pants, thigh high stiletto boots, and a cleavage baring halter top—just right for Peter, doncha think?
>
> **j.p.** . . . or as the Reverend Billy Gibbons so succinctly put it, you're "just looking for some tush." Positively shocking.
>
> **j.c.** Is it bigger than a breadbox?
>
> **j.w.** Is it Peter's Jokebook????
>
> **c.w.** It is Peter's Jokebook.

012809

Peter Carlaftes wants to produce a new TV show called: *I Love Busey* . . .

> **c.f.** That already has my vote for the Most Uncomfortable Half-Hour of Television Emmy.
>
> **f.h.** Now THAT is a good idea!
>
> **j.g.** If you mean Gary Busey, then it's already been done. I'm With Busey was a reality show with the man himself and some kid named Adam Dela Pena, about three years ago on Comedy Central. But if that's not who you meant . . .
>
> **l.e.** That show was hysterical.
>
> **p.m.** I think it should just be a camera following Busey around. Very low budget.
>
> **t.s.** Or an animated show. "Daddy, there's a Busey under my bed!"
>
> **c.b.** best mug shot photo ever!
>
> **p.m.** Maybe Mike Judge can animate it or do the live version also
>
> **t.s.** And James Lipton can be the narrator.

012909

Peter Carlaftes is in the qualm before the storm . . .

> **c.w.** Punmaster flash. Always dependable.

Peter Carlaftes says *Rock the Casbah's* Petty Clash . . .

> **d.m.** sherif don't like it . . .
>
> **p.c.** well, one thing i know that makes death more acceptable is, when it comes, i will never ever have to hear rock the casbah again . . .
>
> **p.m.** don't be too sure
>
> **p.c.** if you got any pull out there in the great beyond, fix it for me not to hear it again—and posthumous thanks . . .
>
> **p.m.** You and me both. although I like The Clash I got sick of that song many years ago.
>
> **d.p.** What's worse, the song or the pun?!
>
> **p.c.** the song, by far . . .
>
> **d.p.** I concede! The song sucks.

013009

Peter Carlaftes has the banking industry's new slogan: *That Goes Without Paying* . . .

> **w.g.** +++

020109

Peter Carlaftes *"What—do you see an ass' head of your own—do you?"* This is the true "Bottom" Line . . .

I assume this means I am without (shakes) peer . . .

> **a.h.** Thou art translanted . . .

Peter Carlaftes is writing a script for the Roy Rogers bio Pic: *You've Got Dale* . . .

> **r.c.** Is that the cat that chewed your new shoes.
>
> **s.g.** Don't forget the episode when Roy lost his sight: Happy Brailles To You.
>
> **r.c.** lol
>
> **p.c.** i'm pissed off at these sons a bitches using my status updates to get bigger laughs than me . . .
>
> **i.k.** i've taken to stealing from your genius. just so you know.

020209

Peter Carlaftes is down to *The Bare Recessities* . . .

> **p.r.** you been watchin mary poppins or somethin?
>
> **p.c.** it *was* The Jungle Book *(*"The Bare Necessities"*)* and these are the bare (r)ecessities soon to be oppressive depressities which could have inspired "Supercalifragilisticexpeallidotious"— so maybe you're right . . .

020309

Peter Carlaftes calls the new Economic policy: *Fill In The Banks* . . .

> **w.g.** ++!
>
> **p.c.** even your ratings are losing value . . .
>
> **w.g.** laughter is increasingly more valuable, in its scarcity

020409

Peter Carlaftes just bought 49 pieces from the Blue Period at Pablo Picostco . . .

YOUR PHOTO HERE

Comment

020609

Peter Carlaftes thinks Michael Phelps just wanted to win one more Gold for Acapulco . . .

> **s.a.** hahahaha
>
> **d.b.** I think Columbia is trying to claim citizenship, too.
>
> **j.g.** maybe the remaining Escobars are trying to form a kick-ass swim team??
>
> **p.r.** He must be swimming in weed! . . . Hey, I'm trying
>
> **c.b.** an Olympian with weed is a friend indeed!
>
> **p.s.** He lost his endorsement from Kellogg's, maybe Dorito's will pick him up now . . . mmmm . . . munchies.
>
> **p.c.** I think he's gunning for a Bud endorsement . . .

Olympic champion swimmer caught sucking a bong . . . Seems somehow out of sync—like . . . Mark Spitz should've been smoking dope in the 70s; Phelps—the goody-goody of the zeros . . . (go figure)

020709

Peter Carlaftes thinks Michael Phelps was smoking pot to promote his new line of swimwear: Weedo . . .

> **j.g.** that's a good. you've got some witty puns my friend.
>
> **s.s.** Whatever he took while promoting speed-o
>
> **j.d.** they should put his face on a box of Weedies cereal.
>
> **t.s.** With some late night advertising, Kelloggs could have cornered the 'munchies' market.
>
> **s.w.** i was right next to him. he bogarted that joint. well maybe he bacalled it.

020809

Peter Carlaftes is gonna live by the Madoff Maxim: *It takes Money—To take Money* . . .

Ponzi-Dude Made-off with double digit billions—later sentenced to triple digit years behind bars.

> **k.h.** I thought the Maxim was if you take the money you Madoff with, you don't get to keep the money you made. Stick to your principles even if you get dirty doing it my friend & your talent will sustain

Peter Carlaftes thinks—that, in these troubled times, we need a new hero: Vincent Half-Price . . .

> **f.t.** Yes, the economy is simply a horror show right now.

021009

Peter Carlaftes is in the cradle of Trivilization . . .

> **w.g.** ! +++ ! (better?)
>
> **p.c.** whew!

021109

Peter Carlaftes thinks—if the Civil War were fought today, the South would stand a chance—because the North's money isn't worth a shit either . . .

Comes a gentle nudge . . .

> **p.r.** you gotta publish this stuff somehow
>
> **p.m.** I think he just did publish it, here. Also, I think this comment thread is only open to people named Peter . . .
>
> **p.n.** If that's the case, then here's my comment too.

> **p.r.** A book of Peter C pop culture related quotes would be great
>
> **p.c.** i'm waiting to field any offers after i take my HGH to make me a better fielder . . .
>
> **s.w.** yes, joe south is formidable and would have prevailed

021209

Peter Carlaftes has developed an antacid for kosher foods called: Al Gefilte . . .

> **w.g.** al? i think i know him, lives on essex? oil gevlet, works, especially after too much schmaltz. i've tried it.

021309

Peter Carlaftes wonders why he has a Feather in his Crap?

> **j.a.** Did you eat something and call it macaroni?
>
> **p.c.** i would hire you j.a., but not to be funny . . .
>
> **j.a.** I'm yer drummer. Rim shots fer hire. :D

021409

Peter Carlaftes to quote old Bill:
*"There lives within the very flame of love . . .
a kind of wick or snuff . . . that will abate it . . ."*

From Hamlet on Valentine's Day . . .

> **p.s.** ha
>
> **n.b.** Oh, when you said 'old bill' I thought you were talking about the police or that guy who founded AA. Double ha.

021609

Peter Carlaftes is going to market a new plastic (biodegradable, of course) replica placesetting called: The Last Tupperware . . .

Still have high hopes for this product . . . Why am I looking up?

> **k.g.** Love it! Could your next product in this line turn water into wine?

021709

Peter Carlaftes is writing a new series about a gentle coroner called: *Carcass Welby* . . .

> **c.f.** Played by Robert Young as he is right now.
>
> **s.w.** carcass welby and his sidekick fore ensic, played by donny osmond. the autopsy twins are dazzling
>
> **s.m.** George Burns plays the carcass!
>
> **p.c.** how about his sidekick is called Topsy and every so often he does that old humble act, Awww, Topsy and off they go to work . . .

021909

Peter Carlaftes thinks if Meryl Streep doesn't win this year, maybe next year in *NunForgiven* . . .

And along come the Oscars . . .

a.l. the devil wears a habit!

c.f. Mamma Superior Mia?

a.l. The Bridges of Vatican County

h.d. Sophie's confession

t.b. Adaptation of the Devil's Choice Confession

a.l. Postcards from the seminary?

c.i. kramer vs. the pope

l.w. Priory Home Companion

a.l. The Manchurian Catholic!

j.g. She-Devil Wears Schmata

n.d. Devout of Africa

and the winner is . . .

022009

Peter Carlaftes thinks if Sean Penn loses this year, he'll win next year for *Bilk: The Bernie Madoff Story . . .*

> **j.k.** HA HA HA HA !!!
>
> **k.h.** THAT IS GREAT
>
> **l.r.** he HAS to win!
>
> **b.b.** Sean Penn is a free soul.
>
> **p.r.** rotfl!
>
> **w.g.** applause applause!
>
> **p.r.** Either Sean or the Mickster I guess. I just hope Mickey doesn't bring his damn mini dogs onstage with him.
>
> **b.b.** Whouafff . . . whouaff!!! . . . Grrrr!!
>
> **k.m.** sean penn already has an oscar. please please give it to mickey rourke!!!

and the winner is not . . .

022109

Peter Carlaftes wants to create a new software program for drug dealers called: *Crystal Math* . . .

> **l.l.** Yeah, it could be like quickbooks for drug dealers, they need help with their finances too.
>
> **p.c.** you're right on the money—now launder it . . .

022209

Peter Carlaftes thinks life's great, until things go from Bad to Hearse . . .

> **c.s.** you funny. i like.
>
> **a.l.** life is short, proust is long!

022309

Peter Carlaftes thinks freedom's just another word for nothing left to choose . . .

> **s.g.** Profound!

Peter Carlaftes asks, Who needs a Cure for Life?

> **a.g.** maybe I found my cure. Eva.
>
> **p.c.** brains, not Braun . . .

022409

Peter Carlaftes says, They give all this money that isn't there to the SOBs that lost all the money that was there—So: Where're those SOBs at that They lost it to?

> **s.m.** So who's the SOBs now that this has been revealed? I'm thinking anarchy.
>
> **s.c.** Some of the SOB's to whom all has been lost were on Teevee tonight, applauding the President (so's not too seem terribly apparent). The rest of 'em are sleeping soundly in beds made of hand-knotted ropes and feathers, dreaming of tomorrow's hookers, triple-malt scotch, and the kiss of warm island breezes. If I had a rocket launcher . . .
>
> **s.m.** SOME SON-OF-A-BITCH WOULD PAY.
>
> **s.c.** http://www.youtube.com/watch?v=N7vCww3j2-w
>
> **s.m.** I didn't know those were the actual lyrics. Good stuff.
>
> **s.c.** ZOMG, that's just one of the best ditties ever, inna?

022509

Peter Carlaftes went to the gym and heard a new version of Rainy Day Woman: *Everybody Must Get Toned* . . .

h.h. NO THEY DIDN'T!

a.l. Bob Dylan's 115th Workout?

p.r. lmao!

022609

Peter Carlaftes thinks—if you can't decide whether you like Crispin or Danny better—then . . . you're "*Torn Between 2 Glovers*" . . .

> **a.l.** I've met them both!
>
> **p.c.** so . . . who's your favorite?
>
> **h.b.** Bruce . . . or John?
>
> **a.l.** hmm . . . tough call I'd say Crispin because he's super awkward! He laughs 5 seconds after every joke. Its almost like he's checking back with his brain to see if what you said was funny. FYI! Don't mention internet piracy! The Dude totally flips out! He becomes so enraged at the thought of someone stealing his work! He went on a 10 min rant about sending this vast army of lawyers to crush the skulls of anyone who ever attempted to steal from him! It was fun funny!
>
> **k.m.** omg! crispin is the best actor of my generation. he's a genius.
>
> **a.l.** I'm a fan of David Thewlis!
>
> **p.r.** Nice!!
>
> **j.h.** hahaaha

Peter Carlaftes says—if you download Ann & Nancy Wilson's music for nothing then . . . *"You're Cheatin' Heart"* . . .

> **j.a.** You are a Magic Man!
>
> **p.c.** for bookings, call my agent Barry Kuda . . .

This bit was from our vaudeville-like show—*Dueling Karaoke*, and if you think you'd like to see it once, well . . . you'd better think twice . . .

PHOTO: MAX CARLAFTES

http://www.youtube.com/3RoomsPress

022709

Peter Carlaftes just saw a sign:
If You Think the System Works,
Just Ask Somebody Who Isn't . . .

> **t.b.** Somebody who isn't works? Artworks? Ironworks?
>
> **m.a.** Isn't working?
>
> **w.g.** who isn't . . . the system . . . they meant well. it's funny and horrifying that whoever wrote that couldn't put it together coherently.
>
> **m.d.** The Revolution Will Not be Grammaticalized
>
> **w.g.** m.d. gets a god star . . .
> (ok i'm leaving that typo)
>
> **m.d.** Will you be sending him via FedEx or will he just be getting off at the bus stop?
>
> **w.g.** ask somebody who isn't
>
> **j.l.** If you think the system IS WORKING, Just ask somebody who isn't.

022809

Peter Carlaftes asks, What next for the Arts? Carnegie Mall?

> **b.f.** Lincoln Shopping Center?
>
> **p.c.** with Central Park-ing?
>
> **p.r.** The Hollywood Bowling Alley
>
> **j.k.** Broadway. Yes, that's all. Broadway.

022909

Peter Carlaftes thinks he bit off more than he could spew . . .

> **t.b.** Naaah! I don't believe it!

030109

Peter Carlaftes just saw a sign: *Please Don't Pee on the Floor; The Maid Has Holes in Her Shoes . . .*

> **j.c.** . . . and you saw the sign just after YOU peed on the floor . . .
>
> **d.n.** You did not!
>
> **m.k.** That is too funny! Where did you see that?
>
> **p.c.** actually, i saw it in the stall of a men's room on the road of rural somewhere—30 years ago . . .
>
> **b.f.** I once saw a sign that said: PLEASE DON'T PEE IN OUR POOL, WE DON'T SWIM IN YOUR TOILET

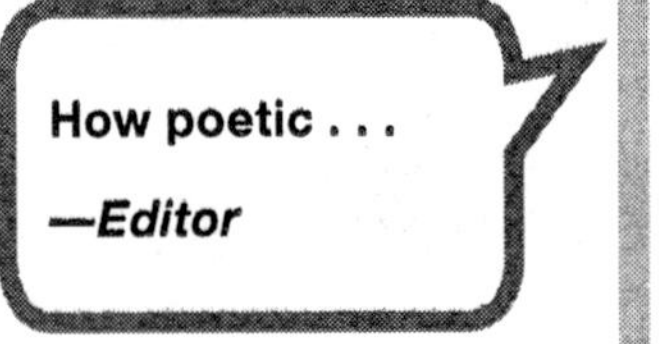

Peter Carlaftes thinks certain Orders of Monks should go through a 12 Steppe Program . . .

> **j.h.** the monk on the mountain and the drunk at the bar both looking for the same thing—a more meaningful interaction with the universe
>
> **p.c.** what did the Dalai Lama say to the hot dog vendor? . . . make me one with everything . . .

030209

Peter Carlaftes is off to Vegas with a surefire system to leave with a small fortune: I'm bringing a large fortune . . .

> **c.y.** last time i was in Vegas i became BFF with the wife of Cinderella's geetar player—really no joke!
>
> **g.d.** roulette system: if it lands on black this time . . . then next time it's bound to be red!

030709

Peter Carlaftes has a real showstopper for the retail sector: *(ta ta ta ta da da) There's No Business . . . Like . . . No Business . . . Like No Business . . . I Know . . .*

YOUR PHOTO HERE

Comment

030809

Peter Carlaftes says—things are really getting bad . . . just saw a homeless Arab panhandler with a sign: *Will Work For Crude* . . .

> **s.g.** oh dear.
>
> **r.g.** :(
>
> **m.s.** :((((
>
> **p.c.** everyone's a critic . . .

And I mean "everyone" . . .

—*Editor*

Peter Carlaftes thinks the Nation's Capitol should reopen as The House of Tax because the figures look so real . . .

> **p.h.** . . . and the joke is . . . ?
>
> **p.c.** let's print up oh say 414 billion dollars . . . why look at that, will you . . . that looks just like a real 414 billion dollars . . . and honey look over there . . . look at that 258 billion dollars over there . . . wow . . . so real . . . some joke—eh?
>
> **p.h.** . . . oops schiezer, that's not a joke, that's comedy. post post potilly—yer swimmin' in it. keep it up.

030909

Peter Carlaftes sings, *It's a Mall World (after all)* . . .

> **s.d.** that's the best one yet.

Since there's not much to keep you, the reader's, children occupied while—you, the reader—read this book, have them log in at ayearonfacebook.com and click on the "Frog" icon to turn it into a "you think you know what"

031009

Peter Carlaftes thinks, it's about time for the adults to start going on PayDates . . . and, like—pretend (you know) there's some money coming in . . .

> **k.d.** LOL . . . Is time!

031109

Peter Carlaftes can't wait to see the season finale of *The Human Race* (as we know it) . . .

031209

Peter Carlaftes is Very Impressed with a new line of vehicles coming out of Holland called: *Mini-Van Goghs . . .*

> **c.c.** hahahahaha :-)
>
> **a.k.** I hear that Belinda Carlisle is going to be the Mini-Van Gogh Gogh's spokeswoman . . . .
>
> **d.g.** now that is funny
>
> **p.c.** yeah . . . well, each one's equipped with a special starry night roof and (though i know i should quit while ahead—here goes): they run on sunflower(s) oil and (forgive me) have these strange ear-view mirrors . . .
>
> **k.c.** you've outdone yourself!

031309

Peter Carlaftes sings *Let's go surfing now, everybody's learning how, click icon safari with me . . .*

YOUR PHOTO HERE

Comment

Peter Carlaftes thinks that conformity has become the new rebellion . . . i mean, how else could you piss off the last generation—except by conforming?

f.m. i wholeheartedly agree . . . like 100%

l.e. bullshit. 100%. sounds like you need new friends.

f.m. ok 110% then.

l.e. i feel like you're calling me a conformist, we might have to brawl.

Hey—Lucky us!
World War Free!

f.m. whatever you like. i'm down for it. 100%. i'll meet you out back of carlaftes' wall at 3:00pm tomorrow.

l.e. i meant what i said and i said what i meant. an elephant's faithful, 100%

f.m. a'ight yo! i was only trying to piss off the last generation initially, but i'll take you to start.

f.m. i feel like this thread needs lots of people commenting with "fight! fight! fight! fight!"

l.e. i just want a hot shower and a cherry fruitpie.

s.m. Could not agree less.

e.b. that's it, i'm pissed

031409

Peter Carlaftes buys all of his Greek specialties at *Deli Savalas . . .*

> **a.z.** who loves u baby
>
> **l.d.** This is awesome.

031509

Peter Carlaftes new series of oscar winning best pictures cum low budget porn: 1) (1938) *Sue Can't Fake It With You . . .*

Peter Carlaftes 2) (1941) *How Clean Was Her Valley . . .*

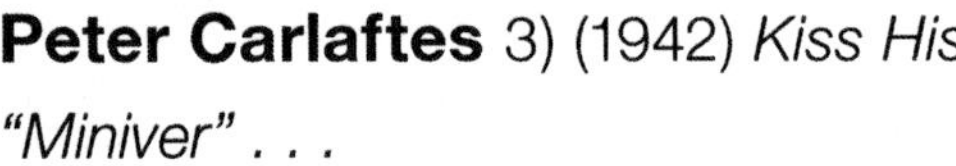

Peter Carlaftes 3) (1942) *Kiss His "Miniver" . . .*

> **b.f.** The Lizard of Mars (1936)
>
> **b.f.** oops—1939 :-0
>
> **b.f.** Dead Liver (1948)
>
> **b.f.** OK—I'LL SHUT UP. Time to go to sleeeepppp zzzzzzz
>
> **a.m.** The Wizzer of Oz (1939)
>
> **j.k.** Saving Ryan's Privates (19??)
>
> **c.c.** the incredible bulk.

Peter Carlaftes 6) (1956) *Around the World (in 80 Ways) . . .*

YOUR PHOTO HERE

Comment

031609

Peter Carlaftes 7) (1959) *Ben(d) Her . . .*

> **c.c.** hahahahahaha :-)
>
> **s.m.** Man this pun is outta my league.

Peter Carlaftes 13) (1981) *Harriet's on Fire . . .*

Peter Carlaftes OK-OK (finis) This one can only be as a double bill . . . 14) (1989) *Driving Sis Crazy* & 15) (2000) *Daddy Ate Her . . .* (whew) . . .

Peter Carlaftes on to next: Dullest Best Picture Winners . . . (1946) *The "Yes, Dears" of My Wife* and (1985) *Out of Paprika*

> **s.w.** out of paprika was meryl streep's most haunting performance, especially in the kitchen scene with soupy sales . . . it just doesn't want to get any better
>
> **a.d.** Brilliant. As most of the time.
>
> **s.m.** You gotta live in NYC to get it maybe? Or maybe i'm just too damn young.
>
> **p.c.** ok s.m . . . how about this . . . (1997) Flytanic about this crazy inventor who builds a great big ship which he believes he can make fly . . . huge wings on the huge ship . . . sir, we're only making 17 knots . . . it'll never leave the water and

become airborne . . . (tagline) Everyone said that it would never work . . . and . . . it never did . . . see Flytanic ok, get it?

s.m. lol

s.w. bebe rebozo is outstanding in flytanic . . . he plays the sick engine . . . montel williams is also remarkable as the drug company bus that drives to the airport when flytanic complains of a stomach upset . . .

s.g. OH MAN!!! THE BEST DEERS OF OUR LIVES!! Bambi's breakout performance. It was Bambi's dramatic turn in this black and white epic that sealed the deal. Disney saw this flick and had to have the young buck in his own cult classic, Bambi & Minnie Do Donald Trump. It swept the 1946 Oscars! An almost unrecognizable Donald Trump with real hair as . . . Thumper Humperdinck, a completely unrecognizable Joan Rivers as Flowerchild Rainforest and a sadly recognizable Rosie O'Donnell as Bambi, Queen of The Forrest Gump! Classic stuff, truly! Many years later The Donald would sell his statuette in an effort to own New York City and sell salsa to New Jersey. Two thumbs up Oscar's butt!

s.m. Planet of the Shapes. A very weird work of fiction, staring no one. It mainly consisted of props bumping one another. Eventually the director had to pull a Deux Ex Machina. As Carrot Topless was being lowered into the scene to sing the final score, her weight proved too much for the crane and it broke leaving her to fall on her neck. Credit Rolls. The f**king end.

p.c. there's also (1931) Simmer On . . . about the man who invented the crock pot way of cooking 40 years before his time and the only recognition he ever got was when he moved his family out west (from wheeling to waco) and slaughtered them and cooked them all very slowly though he was still prosecuted after he died and got 140 years but some thought it was a waste of state money . . . it later became the ferber act, whereas no one can be prosecuted for a crime after death . . . that's all left up to the good lord or whatever else they might call the supreme being up there . . .

031709

Peter Carlaftes OK . . . Final/Final . . .
Silliest Best Picture Winner . . . (1990)
Manson With Wolves . . .

> **p.c.** here, charles manson finds that no one will listen to him and he has no control over anybody and no one will follow him so he wanders off into the desert and then the great plains where he meets these wolves that do listen and follow him and the wolves carry out his evil orders and even attack the president twice after he's been incarcerated . . . hey, what can you say . . . when it's your destiny it's your destiny . . .
>
> **b.w.** This could have been his plan #2. A Wolf Manson. I was at his trial, it is hard to believe he had mind control over anyone though sadly true. The Wolf would be too smart for him!

031809

Peter Carlaftes how do you know who's the bride or groom at a same sex marriage ceremony? they altar-nate . . .

> **r.k.** Groan! :)
>
> **p.r.** ouch . . .
>
> **p.s.** *rimshot*
>
> **m.m.** I wonder if you know, Peter, how many times you make me laugh out loud with your status updates. Guess it doesn't matter. Just keep me laughing, please. :)
>
> **p.c.** everything matters . . . especially laughter—thanks . . .
>
> **j.r.** The groom wears flannel

Peter Carlaftes dullest play ever: *Gorky and Hesse . . . Herman, it's Summertime . . . and Siberia's still freezing . . . well my dear friend Maxim, it's very nice on the Rhine . . .*

I had very high hopes for this *Porgy and Bess* bit but others curbed their (you know what) . . .

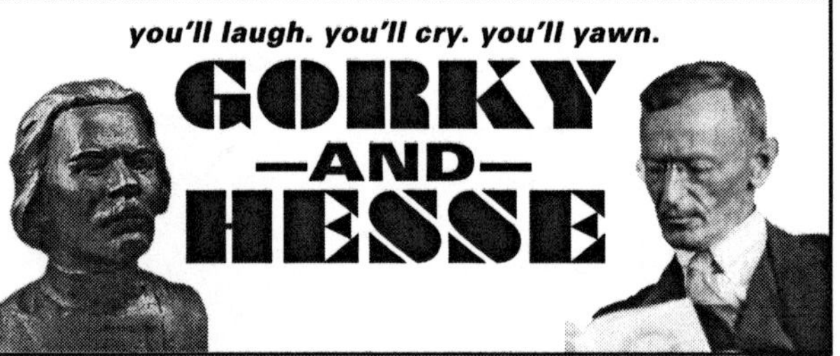

Peter Carlaftes just realized that poor fellow in Iraq was really a shoe-icide bomber . . .

That journalist had thrown a shoe at Bush—so . . .

s.a. Hope ur saving these!

s.g. But seriously folks . . . take my life, please! Thank you, thank you. Tonight, we have a really big shoe for you! So now, without any further mildew . . . on with the shoe!

l.j. silly

i.k. 2 shoes walk into a bar.

p.r. prably he's got fungicide, no shoeicide.

d.w. that pun was soul destroying!

s.g. Fungicide hotline, may I help you? Yes . . . yes . . . uh huh. Right . . . right . . . Don't do it, don't toss your mushrooms over, there's absolutely no reason to believe that your mushrooms are tripping without you.

s.m. OOhahaha fundamental Shoedeism

s.g. With soundtrack by that hot all girl band from the east . . . Shoe 'n Knife!

c.c. hahahaha . . . speaking of shonen knife, i used to be into their music.

031909

Peter Carlaftes just took the "What bad, horribly mean tyrant are you?" quiz and the result is: Idi Amin . . .

> Thus began the phony facebook quiz series . . . (as if there weren't enough real ones)

s.w. you mean forest whitaker or yaphet kotto

p.c. the real mother for you . . .

s.w. t.c. boyle has a great short riff about a dada party in which everyone has to bring something . . . dadaesque . . . and somebody brings idi amin dada . . . i guess dada lived somewhere in his name . . . love these quiz parodies you got going . . . they almost had me fooled . . .

Peter Carlaftes just took the "What fantastical, biblical relic are you?" quiz and the result is: the jawbone of an ass . . .

l.b. A former Prime Minister of my country had and was one of those!

r.c. Lol, that's good.

a.j. hehe . . . mighta been worse, though . . . you coulda ended up with the mess of potage.

> It was worse—ending up with a.j.'s response . . .

032009

Peter Carlaftes just took the "Which stealth missile are you?" quiz and the result is: the one in Dick Cheney's wheelchair . . . (is there such a thing as a stealth missile?)

> **s.g.** Please clarify: stealth missile or stealth missal? The former is obvious; the latter suggests Cheney is secretly saying his prayers (unlikely). :)
>
> **p.c.** give me your exact location and i'll let you know within the hour . . .
>
> **s.g.** Uh, I think the deadline—accent on dead—for delivery of a stealth missile is 15 minutes. Thanks for the heads down; next stop: smithereens! :)

Peter Carlaftes just took the "Which Bernie Madoff (out of 51 billion) purloined dollar are you?" quiz and the result is: dollar # 4,564,751,111 . . .

> **j.p.** purloined is such a great word—only gentlemen purloin—

032109

Peter Carlaftes took the "Which famous German pub drinking song are you?" quiz and the result is: None . . .

> **s.s.** There's a story that Finnish National Anthem was first a German drinking song . . . well, hooray to Mr. Pacius anyways, he's now 200 years!
>
> **j.p.** i would have pegged you as "O Alte Burschenherrlichkeit"

Peter Carlaftes just took the "Which identifiable symbol of hatred are you?" quiz and the result is: The Peace Sign . . .

> **r.c.** Well it's confirmed then, now to play with that Russian Roulette pistol. What! No bullets, damn.

Peter Carlaftes just took the "What chamber of the 6 shot revolver is the bullet in for this round of Russian Roulette?" quiz and the result is: Chamber #4 . . .

> **b.f.** hahaha . . .

Peter Carlaftes just took the "Which life-threatening medical procedure are you?" quiz and the result is: Bone Marrow Transplant . . .

> **c.s.** This is hands-down the funniest status I have read! Damn near gave me a brain freeze.
>
> **k.g.** you slay me
>
> **j.e.** Yes, these are good jokes . . .
>
> **c.c.** hahahahaha so funny! love reading your status' . . .
>
> **c.s.** okay, I'm still laughing
>
> **s.w.** carlaftes, the ambulance is on its way . . . don't despair . . . moe, larry and curley joe have the secret elixir . . . drink 2 large glasses and then sing the national anthem backwards . . . why aren't you the secretary of humor in the new cabinet?

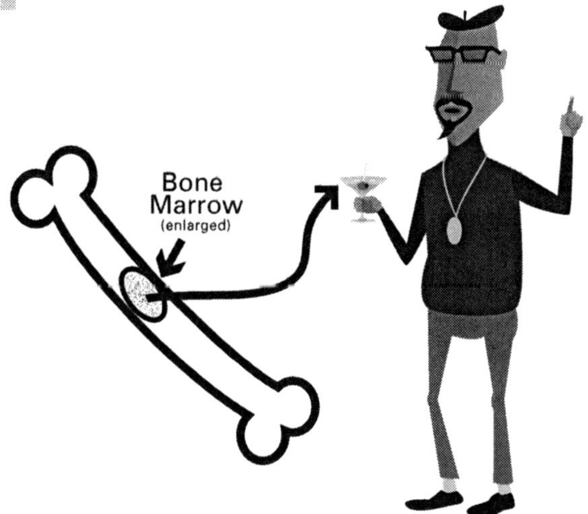

032209

Peter Carlaftes is watching new reality show: *Same-Ex Marriage* . . .

> **a.g.** How come nobody thought about a reality show where exes live in a loft together?

Peter Carlaftes just saw the worst reality show ever; about going out with a dweeb called: *Alexander the Date* . . .

Maybe Alexander had a little too much on his date . . .

Peter Carlaftes is, after jumping a barbed-wire fence on a motorcycle, going to brunch at *The Greatest Crepe* . . .

> **c.s.** you're killing me!
>
> **r.g.** that is funny!
>
> **k.w.** LOL

032309

Peter Carlaftes just sent a *Marv Albert bites Lana Turner's daughter's red panties while reglueing his toupee Orangina Bottle* to all AIG execs as a Q1 bailout bonus . . .

> **Editor** ☐ Block this Application

Peter Carlaftes just have all those wall street bailout bigs come and get their bonus checks inside the Roman Coliseum . . . (it'd be the "Christian" thing to do) . . .

> **k.g.** clear as a bell.
>
> **p.r.** that would rule. Too bad theres no more public stonings :(
>
> **p.p.** i thinks they deserve more . . .

Peter Carlaftes you know, Aesop really brought a lot to the Fable . . .

> **c.b.** very punny!
>
> **b.c.** i like you

Peter Carlaftes saw a great spinoff band called Cheap Truck who sing: *I Want You . . . to Jump Me . . .*

> **d.n.** Not nearly as romantic as the original.

032409

Peter Carlaftes is listening to French pop: Celine Dijon (ouch: that must-hurt) . . .

> **p.s.** My favorite mutard!
>
> **d.g.** The singing Q-Tip
>
> **p.r.** sorry but i'm lol @ mutard
>
> **c.c.** hehehehe :-) classic . . . keep 'em comin' !

Peter Carlaftes you know, Paul McCartney & Stevie Wonder are planning a new album called: *Songs in the Key of Live and Let Die* . . .

> **j.w.** HARF!

Peter Carlaftes and now, kids—give
a big hand to German's Hermits . . .
Ich bin Henreich sie Acht Ich bin . . .

> **a.k.** with hits like . . . "I'm into something gut" . . . "No beer today" . . . "Just a little bit bitter" and last but not least, their world war 2 hit . . . "There's a Rhine-like push, all over the world" groan
>
> **j.g.** "Liebensraum, you've gotterdam a lovely daughter"
>
> **g.h.** "I'm Henried the Reich I am"
>
> **r.s.** Those guys actually played my town about 12 yrs back. I love that track: Es gibt eine Art von Hush (überall auf der Welt). I used to think Henreich stole it from The Carpenters, but they both stole it from someone else.

032509

Peter Carlaftes you could always pair up Diamond and Garfunkel: *"I Am A Rock I Said"* . . .

> **p.b.** mega!
>
> **c.b.** nice conceptually!

Peter Carlaftes then again, there's the great duet of Simon and Bullwinkle; just sing *"Me and Julio"* to the Bullwinkle theme . . .

> **f.c.** You, Sir, are one demented mammajamma. Bravo.
>
> **n.d.** Or Simon and Kilmer, who sang "You Can Call Me Val"
>
> **k.m.** Simon Smith and the Amazing Dancing Yogi Bear. Sorry, I tried.

Peter Carlaftes and, finally—the last coupling . . . Simon and Simon and Garfunkel: *"Loves Me Like I Am A Rock"* . . .

> **p.r.** New detective show where a mathematician solves the cases . . . the title: Magnum Pi

032609

Peter Carlaftes has a new animated series for the ages: *Clintstones . . . Meet the Clintstones . . . They are Quite the Politically-Driven Family . . .*

> **s.w.** with clint walker, clint eastwood, clint ritchie, clint howard, clinton sundberg, clint black, lewis stone, oliver stone, sharon stone, like a rollin' clintstone, i'll kill you with my telephone just like in the end of fuller's the naked kiss, when you're a clint stone you're living in bliss . . .
>
> **p.c.** and just watch as the neighbor kid comes by to mess up their perfect world . . . Bam Bam . . . Bam Bam . . .

032709

Peter Carlaftes just downloaded new recording: *Dick Cheney Sings Jim Morrison . . . Well, I woke up this morning and I shot myself a De-er. . .*

> **t.u.** Ok, that made me laugh through my nose on sight . . .
>
> **p.c.** Spit-take . . . Quite an honor . . .

032809

Peter Carlaftes let's 21st Centurize the punk movement w/The Safe-Sex Pistols—w/Yid Vicious & Connie Rotten . . .

> **m.d.** There's actually a decent klezmer band from Madison WI called Yid Vicious: www.yidvicious.com
>
> **c.c.** hahahahaha :-)

Peter Carlaftes just had his brunch money stolen on the playground of facebook . . .

> **t.m.** That's almost Orwellian in nature.

Peter Carlaftes is well along the way from fetal to fatal . . .

> **a.k.** is that like after birth?
>
> **s.c.** Oh, cheer up. You think I want
> to depend on you in the foxhole?
> Viva la revolucion.
>
> **p.c.** what's la revolucion? some album you like?

032909

Peter Carlaftes just took the "Which 20th Century Band are You?" quiz and the result is: The frequency band for FM radio at about 88 to 108 MHz . . .

> **b.b.** Stereo-typing?
>
> **e.m.** What's the frequency?
>
> **d.w.** if only everyone was on your wavelength . . .

Peter Carlaftes took the "What's your Mafia Name?" quiz and the result is: You got a problem with that?

> **h.p.** Always there to upturn a Monday, Tues, Weds frown!
>
> **p.c.** so what am i dirt on thursday?

Q. What's your mafia name?
A. You got a problem with that?

I'd done a bit called Christ on a Crossword Puzzle and these were some of the jokes (a kinder/gentler outcome) . . .

033109

Peter Carlaftes time for Easter jokes: What did the one weary Centurion say to the other after fending off the crowd around Jesus's cell? . . . Thank God It's Friday . . .

> **r.c.** Ha, you nailed that one.

Peter Carlaftes Easter Joke #2: What's the quickest way to contact Jesus? . . . E-nail . . . 2nd quickest way? . . . CruciFax Machine . . .

> **j.e.** wheeee-oooooo.
>
> **p.s.** Ouch!
>
> **w.a.** 2,000 years and this is all you've got?
>
> **w.d.** I'll save a place in hell for you haha

040109

Peter Carlaftes Easter #3: What did Paul say to Jesus when he saw him Resurrected? . . . Jeez—What Happened? You look like you just crawled out from under a rock . . .

> **s.c.** omg . . . going to hell, lol!
>
> **k.d.** hahaha!!!
>
> **j.k.** Easter #4: Jesus Christ walks into a hotel, lays 3 nails on the counter, and says to the innkeeper, "Can you put me up for the night?"
>
> **m.h.** Luckily the J man always seemed like he had a sense of humor.
>
> **g.b.** hilarious!
>
> **s.g.** brother, you are on a roll!!! now, if we could just get some mustard, a kosher slice . . . some ham. oh wait, got plenty of ham . . . cheese? yep, got plenty of that too!

040209

Peter Carlaftes Easter #5: What did the waiter say to Jesus upon presenting the check for the Last Supper? "Bless You—Come Again . . ." What did Jesus say after picking up the check? "Next Time, They'll Pay . . ."

> **m.d.** yukkety yuk yuk.
>
> **w.a.** Is this divided equally between 12? Judas, what did you have? Come back here! What do you reckon Thomas? You don't think this is right? Peter, I've asked you three times. Did you have a starter?

040309

Peter Carlaftes Easter #7: What did Jesus say to Peter standing at the foot of the cross? "It's not bad, once you get the hang of it . . ."

> **p.b.** Oh, I'll steal that, I will
>
> **j.g.** he also said, "hey! I can see your house from here!"
>
> **s.w.** and now for my next number . . . and peter said no cross and jesus said just find me the girl and peter said how much more money do you need and jesus said i'm buying the future mr. paul and mrs.paul, paul's common law wife, she said i'll put some fishsticks on
>
> **d.w.** dig it.
>
> **c.w.** Groan.
>
> **k.m.** I could a had a V8!

040409

Peter Carlaftes Easter #8: What did they first call the garment Jesus was crucified in? . . . The Shroud of Urine . . . (hey, you hold it in three days) . . .

> **t.c.** When will Jesus bring the Pork Chops?
>
> **k.m.** Oh my sides! You people are hilarious!

Peter Carlaftes . . . Easter #9: What did Jesus say to his Mother Mary kneeling at the foot of the cross? "Look Ma . . . No Hands . . . "

> **a.k.** It's alright Ma, I'm only bleeding . . . (zimmerman)
>
> **s.g.** dude, you really should put these altogether and do a quick easter tour . . . these jokes kill!
>
> **r.c.** I thought he said "Spend the life insurance on real estate."
>
> **w.d.** OMG, You definetly have a place reserved in hell . . . see ya there . . . lol
>
> **s.g.** save me a seat in the corner.

040509

Peter Carlaftes Easter #15: Name the Most Famous Easter Carol circa 33 a.d.: *"Here Comes Jesus Caught-On-Nails"*

> **p.r.** probly wasn't "hoppin" too well eh?

040609

Peter Carlaftes OK/OK—Easter #17: What did John the Baptist have to say to Jesus before Every hand of Poker? "Ante-Christ . . . "

Peter Carlaftes (Ding-Ding/Final One) Easter #18: What did John the Baptist tell Jesus while they were Playing Poker? . . "I'll See your Crown of Thorns and Raise you Three Days Later . . . "

> **m.m.** This is SO bad, it's actually SO good! Thanks. :)
>
> **t.f.** you're a nut job . . . i mean that in a good way
>
> **j.h.** Of course, old John didn't have a head at the time, but . . .

040709

Peter Carlaftes just took the "What is your Hippie Name" quiz and the result is: "You still owe me 10 bucks for 2 lids, Man. . ."

> **e.l.** That's one hell of a deal . . .
>
> **c.f.** It called me a narc.
>
> **e.l.** No lids for you.
>
> **c.c.** hahahahahahahahaha
>
> **a.g.** 10 bucks for 2 lids? Them wuz days, man.
>
> **j.s.** lids!
>
> **c.b.** I remember when a lid was 10 bucks!

040809

Peter Carlaftes is only listening to (Kosher Frank) Sinatra . . .

> **k.g.** does he come with kosher mustard and kosher coke on the side?
>
> **p.c.** I did it B'nai Way . . .
>
> **p.s.** That's a good one.

040909

Peter Carlaftes . . . How many Obama supporters does it take to change a light bulb? . . . Doesn't matter . . . Just as long as there is Change . . . (Wait! Did he say something Wrong?)

Well? Did he?

—Editor

041009

Peter Carlaftes Thank Good It's Friday . . .

> **j.d.** I wonder if Jesus would agree with you. ;-) It's going to be a looong friday.
>
> **j.c.** Well, the FIRST good Friday kinda sucked, but since then, not so bad.
>
> **c.w.** I'm so jealous you have a friend named Jesus Chryst. I hope he's on Twitter.
>
> **g.d.** today and xmas are the days i disagree with the separation of church and state.

041109

Peter Carlaftes dear peter . . . an image is the presence of an absence . . . sincerely yours, physics . . .

> **c.f.** At least it wasn't addressed to "Current Resident."

041209

Peter Carlaftes if you want someone to blame for our dreams not coming true (except to be sold in this world at a price): Fault Disney . . .

Use your Technicolor Sharpie to edit this one!

041309

Peter Carlaftes figured out that ATM stands for: *At The Mercy* . . .

> **j.j.** . . . and I have noticed for me these days it means "Aint That Much" is gonna spitting out for my retrieval.
>
> **c.b.** ahhh, er, ahem . . . not according to google, lol!

041409

Peter Carlaftes that's like the Goth calling the Metal "slack" . . .

> **d.w.** Or a frog calling a toad ugly . . . as one your cute little American Presidents once said some decades ago . . .

041709

Peter Carlaftes could it be Status Night (and the pips)?

> **s.d.** My people say Oy Vey. That's bad. So bad it's okay.

042009

Peter Carlaftes has a new rehash of old sitcom: *MisTourette . . . A horse is a horse—* Bullshit!—*of course . . . talk to MisTourette* . . . (who knows . . . tune in next week . . . maybe he can be cured) . . .

> **j.e.** my ribs hurt after that one.

Have a short script for Will Ferrell as Wilbur . . .

042309

Peter Carlaftes watch the new auto-bio-doc about that great Monty Python luminary . . . *I'm-Eric-An-Idle* . . . (get it? get it? do you get it—huh?)

> **m.d.** I had to hit "Like" so I could write "boo" in this little box. Boo, hiss.
>
> **e.b.** ouch!
>
> **d.b.** that's so gear.

I Googled "gear" and got Grandpa Walton . . . then Yahooed "gear" and got *Nights in Rodanthe*—yuk . . .

The editor believes this blurb is a bit obtuse—or an obtuse bit.
(ed.—It's getting more obtuse.)
(p.c.—Let me explain. Goggled "gear"—got "Will Geer." Yahooed "gear"—got "Richard Gere.")
(ed.—Don't confuse the reader.)
(p.c.—how about the writer?).

042509

Peter Carlaftes . . . hereby dubs the modern breed of unaccountables: *Fauxseurs* . . . so "nothing"—they're not even "real" poseurs . . . They are *Fauxseurs* . . .

> **j.l.** Absolutely!
>
> **t.h.** Excellent. I have known a few of these.
>
> **d.w.** And its all administered by a Mockcuracy—has rules and regulations but people still do just what they like that will benefit only them.
>
> **w.v.** No mo fauxseurs fo sho! Either you're born to pose or you're not! Be a real poser . . . like me! :-)

042709

Peter Carlaftes since the world began now, let us commemorate that great inventor: Alexander Graham Cell . . .

> **p.r.** haha!
>
> **c.b.** where do you find the time?
>
> **p.c.** usually on the face of a clock . . .

042809

Peter Carlaftes . . . here's to all parents who talk down to their kids but still want to be informative: *This little piggy went to Green Market, This Little Piggy went to his Solar-Powered home; This little piggy had grass-fed free range Roast Beef, and this little piggy had swine flu and he covered his mouth completely when he coughed . . .*

043009

Peter Carlaftes just took the "Which grade would you give Obama after his first 100 days?" quiz and the result is: . . . Sixth. (Hey, I printed up a lot of worthless paper that year, too!)

One thing I learned on Facebook is this: Obama laughs are harder to come by than belly laughs at a pro-choice rally . . . (more silence) (and) from those who get it . . . (even more silence) . . .

050509

Peter Carlaftes just took the "Which Pre-Mesozoic Era ossified fossil are you?" quiz and the result is: Pia Zadora . . .

> **t.d.** LOL—but she has money!!!
>
> **b.f.** Hahahaaaa!
>
> **m.p.** Ah no no no no.
>
> **m.m.** I would have pegged you as Charo. How wrong would I have been? :)

050609

Peter Carlaftes would like to adopt Madonna . . . any suggestions?

> **j.e.** I think you should really try it. Do a press release and everything. I will keep my eye on the headlines!
>
> **j.g.** you might wanna sanitize her before you let her in your house
>
> **p.s.** Marry her and divorce her and you'll be rich. I believe Guy Ritchie walked off with $95 million.
>
> **j.j.** Be nice to Madonna, she has been through a lot. Cuddle her at night. Whisper her your prayers. In the morning, make her fresh orange juice. Rub her little Madonna feet. Try a little tenderness.
>
> **j.c.** hypnotize her with a diamond rosary
>
> **l.b.** Raise your expectations. Guy Ritchie could give you some pointers that aren't part of her bra.
>
> **l.l.** Watch Body of Evidence before beginning the proceedings.

050709

So . . . Let's go the other way . . .

Peter Carlaftes has decided to put Madonna up for adoption . . . Any takers?

> **j.e.** Foster care might straighten her out.
>
> **b.f.** Can I force her to wear incontinence pants?
>
> **c.w.** Force her, there's a good chance she dons them as we speak.
>
> **b.f.** And I'm kitting her up with a menopause guidance counsellor
>
> **c.w.** She's got to have at least a couple of those on staff already.
>
> **p.c.** jeez, and i thought those hot flashes were pyrotechnics . . .
>
> **p.p.** Nah . . . I'd rather adopt a high voltage electric fence—more talent and personality . . .

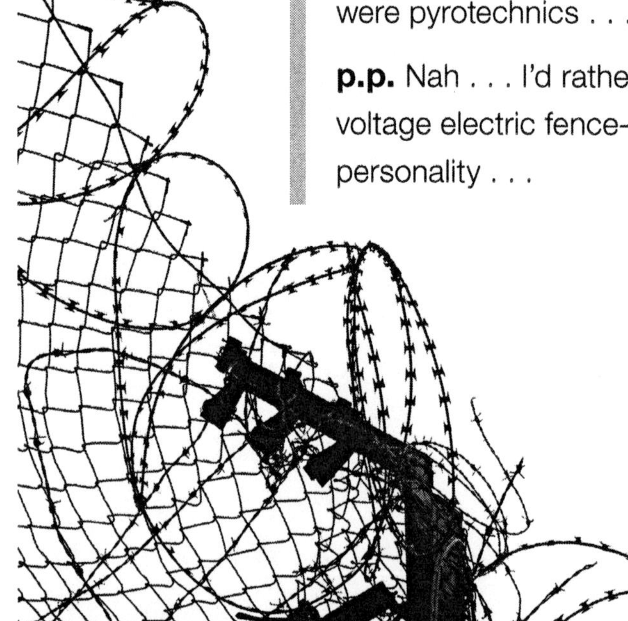

050909

Peter Carlaftes Since it's all the rage, why not give performance enhancing drugs to the economy?

> **r.n.** sorry, not covered by the senate's HMO
>
> **g.b.** haha. I'll sign that petition.
>
> **j.j.** Another good reason to invest in Merck Pharmaceuticals, maker of the little blue pill.

051309

Peter Carlaftes is opening a new document removal service called: *The Grateful Shred* . . .

> **s.d.** terrible.
>
> **c.w.** Groan.
>
> **b.f.** man oh man oh man
>
> **j.j.** Good name for a cheese factory.
>
> **c.c.** hahahahaha, like it !

051709

Peter Carlaftes has a new song to sing to your none-too-willing date: *Com-ply With Me . . . Come On—Let's Go . . . Comply . . .*

> **h.g.** Reminds me of the snake in Jungle Book . . .
>
> **l.j.** come cry, come die, come sigh, come stick it in your eye with me
>
> **p.h.** . . . it's weak, try this: "Well on the way, alone on a hill, the man of a thousand voices keeping perfectly still, they don't won't to know him, they can see that he's just a stool, they don't understand him, but the stool on the hill, sees the world turning round, and the eyes in his head . . . "
>
> **p.c.** of the 3 responses p.h.—I'd have to give you turd place . . .
>
> **m.m.** Oh, great. Now that song's gonna be stuck in my head all day. Com-ply with me, come ply, let's ply away. Thanks a lot. :)

052009

Peter Carlaftes asked the waitress to bring me a steak and a few kind words. She brought me the steak. I said, "What are the kind words?" She said, "Don't eat the steak . . . "

Great Leonard Barr shtick (Dean Martin's uncle) . . .

> **s.a.** Ha!

Peter Carlaftes told the waitress to tell the chef to take the steak and shove it down his throat, and she came back and said, "I'm sorry, sir—but there's two orders of lamb chops ahead of yours . . . "

> **j.e.** Youch!

052209

Peter Carlaftes just read a very scathing exposé of torture and abuse by Castro's wife called: *Commie Dearest* . . .

> **w.c.** good stuff.

052609

Peter Carlaftes hates to be a downer—but . . . *The End is Rear* . . .

> **m.m.** Are you sure it's not in arrears? Never mind. I always get that confused. :)
>
> **m.w.** my end's not in my ears . . . oh ARRears . . . thought you said HER ears . . . ;-)))
>
> **h.h.** That's what she said . . .
>
> **s.r**. Once people figure out the shadows on cave walls they'll stop this "end is near" crap

052709

Peter Carlaftes thinks it all has gotten out of politically correct hand—since he just saw a sign which read: *Vandal With Care* . . .

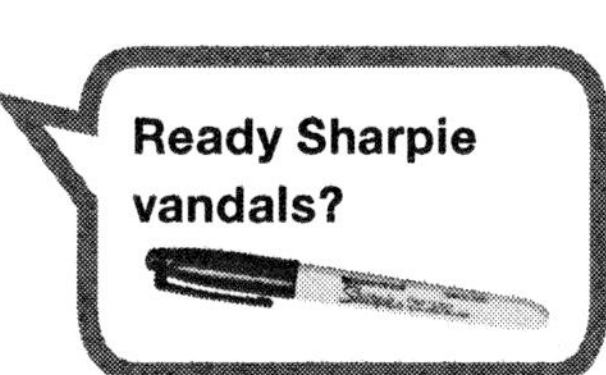

052809

Peter Carlaftes is starting a new Website devoted to Celebrity Club Sightings called: *The Young and the Guest List* . . .

> **j.e.** that's really funny

Peter Carlaftes Nobody knows this—But Warhol was totally misquoted . . . Andy was really barbecuing out in the Hamptons when he said, Every *steak* gets its 15 minutes of *"Flame"* . . .

> **s.r.** I think he was at a drag bar.

052909

Peter Carlaftes just realized that conformity is not the new rebellion; *Uniformity* is the new rebellion . . .

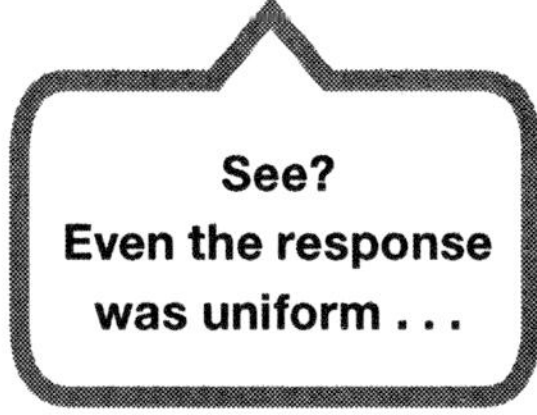

053109

Peter Carlaftes just saw an ad for Penis Enhancement called *Maxiderm* and thought—Hey, if they want to do this right, Why not call it: *Pachsyderm* . . . (you know, like an elephant trunk? Dude!)

> **r.m.** that is so funny!
>
> **g.d.** what did the elephant say to the naked man? "how do you pick peanuts up with THAT?"
>
> **a.k.** and you'll wind up with a penis that never forgets

060409

Peter Carlaftes can see that—A Traitor is someone that Goes With the Foe . . .

> **s.r.** . . . instead of "the flow."

060709

Peter Carlaftes has rewritten a semi-old standard into a new anthem for the ranks of unemployed called: *The Pay We Were* . . .

> **c.b.** Clever and true!

061009

Peter Carlaftes OMG . . . TMI -FYI . . . LMFAO . . . :)))))))))))))))))))))))) . . . WTF . . .

> **t.h.** Indeed.

061209

Peter Carlaftes is ready for *The People's Quart* . . . (Johnny Walker Black)

> **p.r.** i hear ya!
>
> **d.w.** JWB? Nah! Its a Macallan's for me!
>
> **j.c.** cry me a liver
>
> **p.r.** wild turkey for me!

061609

Peter Carlaftes How about this? So their name is The Fetals (instead of The Beatles) and how many songs can you name? . . . "*The Long and Winding Cord*." How many Fetals songs can you name?

> **p.h.** We all live in a yellow uterus? ugh.
>
> **m.a.** Baby Madonna
>
> **p.h**. Fool on the Pill.
>
> **l.h.** Lucy in the Womb with Fluid.
>
> **j.m.** Hey Brood
>
> **l.w.** "Here comes your son"
>
> **m.h.** We Can Push It Out.
>
> **s.s.** . . . baby you can drive my car . . .
>
> **s.m.** there's a placenta, oh bla dee OBGYN, happiness is a warm speculum, do you want to know a secretion, all you need is gloves, within you then without you, flexing a hole, man you're a rich baby, you know my name (you made it up), etc.
>
> **s.s.** I am the egg cell, I am the egg cell, I am the embryo!

l.w. in my wife*

r.l. Some work just as is: Let It Be (Pro-Choice); Doctor Robert; Help! (woman in labor); A Hard Day's Night (ditto); I Should Have Known Better (ditto); Another Girl (Octo-Mom); Come Together (what caused the trouble to start with); Here comes the Son (Octo-Mom again); Golden Slumbers (count back from 100) . . .

m.a. Why Did We Do It in the Road

v.l. My Sweet Cord

j.l. Give Birth a Chance . . .

v.l. I wanna hold your scan

j.l. Across the Uterus, Birth Naturally, It won't be long labor, Long tall episiotomy, Got to get your into my birth canal, back in the obgyn's office, a hard day's labor, honey don't (push just yet), here comes the crown, I am the uterus

***In My Wife* was my personal favorite . . .**

061809

Peter Carlaftes How about "Silly" Joel Songs? . . . Like: *Hey—I'm the Keanu Man . . . and My Last Name is Reeves . . .*

> **p.s.** don't forget "Tell Neo about it" and "Sleeping with the Matrix on"
>
> **p.c.** My . . . Third . . . Wife's . . . Moving Out . . .
>
> **t.c.** "Upload Girl."
>
> **s.c.** Watch Out for that Tree!

062009

Peter Carlaftes *. . . Saturday . . . in the Bar . . . I think it was my 4th shot of Rye . . .*

> **m.f.** reminds me of A Fan's Notes . . .
>
> **p.s.** Sounds like a Sinatra song.
>
> **p.c.** It's the Chicago version with brass chuckles . . .

062109

Peter Carlaftes . . . since it is Fathers Day . . . here's to Adam . . . the "real" founding FATHER . . . jeez, must've had some constitution . . . maybe the apple was the original Viagra . . .

> **d.w.** How crap was it in the Garden of Eden that the best thing Eve could find to tempt Adam with was an . . . apple?

062209

Peter Carlaftes can't believe they're putting 200 mattresses in Times Square and allowing legitimately married heterosexual couples to have consensual sex (while trying to get pregnant) right there on The Great White Way . . .

This was a take on NYC filling Times Square with cheap deck chairs—duh?

> **c.y.** what day? Today? Will it be on the View?
>
> **g.d.** monty pythonesque
>
> **p.c.** yeah . . . amazing . . . used to be just live sex in the theaters . . . but—now! . . . jeez . . . anybody wanna buy a bridge?
>
> **c.d.** Can I pay for the bridge in Elbonian Grubnicks?

062309

Peter Carlaftes it was really beyond belief, but down in the morgue . . . Ed just said — *Heeeeeeeeeeeeeeeeeres The Coroner* . . .

> **m.p.** You sick bastard. LOL!!!!!!

Ed MacMahon dies, the first of many in the summer of death . . .

062409

Peter Carlaftes somebody should tell that S.C. Governor—that (next time), he'd better "Buy American" . . .

Poor South Carolina Governor (What's His-Name) got his hand caught in the South American cookie jar . . .

062509

Peter Carlaftes OMG! Michael Jackson, Farah Fawcett and Ahmadinejad dead in one day?

> **h.h.** Who's gonna heal the world now?
>
> **n.s.** Anderson Cooper
>
> **v.m.** terrible
>
> **e.s.** Ahmadinejad dead? what?
>
> **c.m.** you know any other day I wouldn't have actually googled to see if Ahmadinejad somehow did die this day. Good one, you had me.

Could've started like a viral *War of the Worlds* panic!

063009

Peter Carlaftes sssshhhhhhhh . . . I think Death is taking a Holiday weekend . . . Arghhhhh . . . (clutches throat) . . . one day . . .

> **s.g.** Sorry, just found out that Pina Bausch is gone. Death is still on the job.

070109

Peter Carlaftes Everybody tune in to the WWF's *Death Cage Grudge Match* between Revs. Al "Capone" Sharpton and Jesse "James" Jackson for the privilege to eulogize Jacko at his funeral . . . (HBO Pay-Per-View; $19.95) . . .

> **d.p.** hahahahaha solid
>
> **j.s.** for real?
>
> **j.h.** I almost think I'd pay to see that.
>
> **j.h.** I almost think I'd pay to see that.
> ref.: that dude say the same thing 2X

070409

Peter Carlaftes doesn't want to see the Statute of Liberty expire . . .

> **m.k.** Happy 4th of July

070809

Peter Carlaftes can't believe they changed the history books from Armstrong's *"One Small Step"* ditty to now refer to Michael Jackson's *Moonwalk* . . . sheeeesh . . . so long to the King of Pop . . .

070909

Peter Carlaftes jeez . . . L.A. is so broke, The Coroner had to ship back Michael Jackson's brain Postage Due . . . (do they still have postage due?)

071009

Peter Carlaftes . . . Dear Friends, . . . henceforth, I will be defecting to Cuba— So . . . my Staycations will be more awesome than yours . . .

> **t.d.** at least they have good health care there! :-)
>
> **m.k.** I would go for the palm trees, beaches and drinks!!!:)
>
> **d.w.** spent a month in Cuba in 98 and loved it. Viva Cuba! Viva big men with cigars! Viva gorgeous women with bendy dancey legs!

071109

Peter Carlaftes since Guantanamo Bay carries such a stigma, it's name will be changed to *The Surfside Siesta* . . .

071209

Peter Carlaftes . . . *Sunday Will Never Be The Same* . . .

> **j.r.** What's "Sunday" but a counting trick? A state of mind? One more fantasy we pretend is real . . .
>
> **t.i.** I remember children feeding flocks of pigeons
>
> **s.r.** But Sunday is different, somehow . . . Even here in the country the quiet's got a different quality to it.

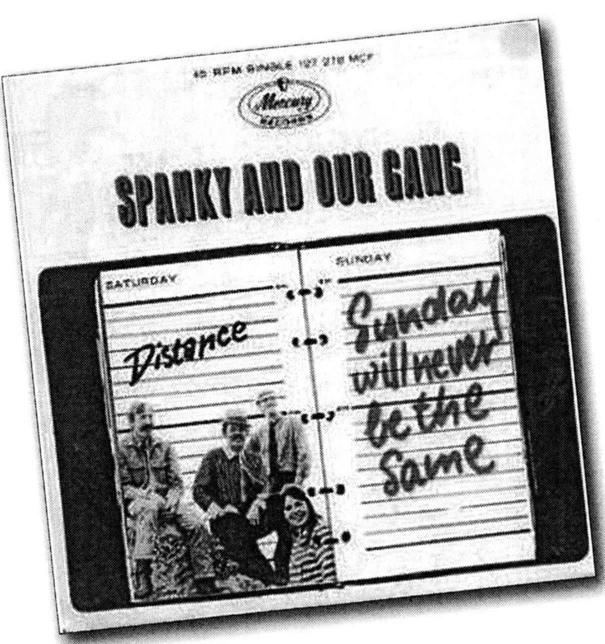

071409

Peter Carlaftes wants to know if someone who steals toilet bowls is a *Septomaniac*?

> **l.w.** A setpomaniac steals things only in sevens. I guess that would include toilets, but it'd be tough logistically to get them all at once.
>
> **t.m.** That guy would be in deep shit, then
>
> **j.c.** Porcelainic?
>
> **t.b.** Is there a 12 step program for them?
>
> **l.m.** There used to be, but some "asshole" made off with steps 1–7.
>
> **a.m.** Simply, yes. yes, they are.
>
> **j.m.** either that or it's someone who thinks it's september all year long . . .

071509

Peter Carlaftes keeps hearing all this misplaced pity about "Ohmless" people . . . so why don't they just take some kind of meditation class, dude?

> **l.m.** It's just so current.

071609

Peter Carlaftes says *Jazz is Like a Drunk who Walks Perfect . . .*

Stole this line from my own play: ***Anti . . .***

t.h. Superb.

c.c. yes!

a.l. oui oui

t.b. well said

071709

Peter Carlaftes hates to jinx it—But, seems like Nobody Somebody's "died" in—Like—Ages . . .

g.d. peter carlaftes RIP

d.g. I'm pullin' for Barbara Walters.

It wasn't me . . .

g.d. SEE WHAT YOU DID?!!! walter cronkite RIP! you rotton old sod!

t.i. You. Killed. Walter.

s.m. way to go douchebag. rip walter.

m.a. how could you . . .

Really . . .

t.b. Are we taking requests ?

072009

Peter Carlaftes is gonna go catch a Buzz with a Collins at Armstrongs and celebrate the 40th anniversary of when they didn't really land on the moon . . .

072209

Peter Carlaftes . . . did you know that 100 years from now—this day (for reasons unknown) will be the first (of many) Aston Kutcher Days . . . Believe it (or don't) . . .

p.r. that's no good

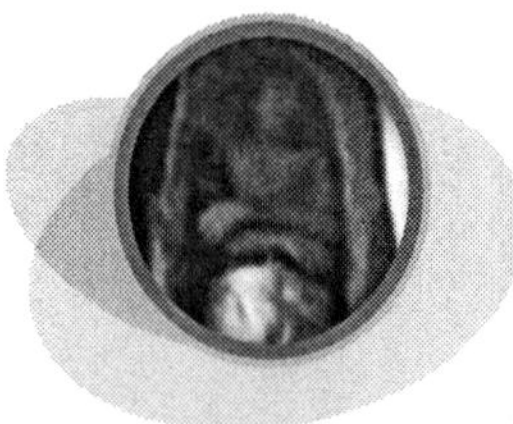

Here, keep in line with the myriad number of celebrity dead. Click on the above crypt icon every Monday to see each week's pick of Who Dies Next. Log in to ayearinfacebook.com for more details.

072409

Peter Carlaftes Since everybody's out of work, the new idiom must be: *Bank Card It's Friday . . .*

072509

Peter Carlaftes just loves the "millions for defense but not one cent for tribute" band . . . Stockman Turner OverDraft's: *"Faking Shares of Business"* . . .

Since the old FB folk added the thumbs up (Like) symbol fewer respond with words . . .

072809

Peter Carlaftes is going to open an oral hygiene outlet called: Bad, Breath and Beyond . . .

> **m.p.** Drink some coffee. That'll kill da bad breath!

072909

Peter Carlaftes wonders, if a mummy really came back to life . . . would it read from Left to Rot?

> **l.w.** Yes, but very sloughly.
>
> **p.r.** what kind of gift do you buy a mummy? some sort of more cohesive garment maybe, but a mummy might not care . . . difficult to say. any ideas?
>
> **p.c.** perhaps something by either of the Russian designers Sarkoff or Ghuss . . .

073009

Peter Carlaftes is, given this pitiable economy, tired of waking up on the wrong side of the bread . . .

080109

Peter Carlaftes has designed a new line of overalls for older women called: Saggety Ann . . .

Call the men's line: Not So Randy . . .

080209

Peter Carlaftes would much rather be able to "Spend" it like Beckham . . .

> **d.w.** Eh? Posh or the stupid one?

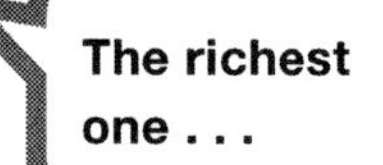

080309

Peter Carlaftes thinks there might be some way to text message the lifeguard listening to their ipod when you're drowning . . .

> **k.z.** Yeah, or relay an electrical shot into his ear!

080409

Peter Carlaftes . . . Jesus comes back to Earth just to check things out in 44 a.d. and sees some other cat having a tough time carrying a cross, so he gives the guy a hand and when the fellow thanked him—Jesus says, Hey—that's just how I was raised . . . (rim shot: easter joke number 23; a little late, use it next year) . . .

I was pleased to come up with a new Easter Joke!

> **k.g.** LOL!!!!!
>
> **r.h.** you know the one with the m&m's?
>
> **p.c.** did they fall through the holes in his hands?
>
> **r.h.** that's the one!

080509

Peter Carlaftes How do you say *Ménage à Trois* in Korean? . . . (how do you say it in English, for that matter?)

Mr. Clinton saved the journalists . . . Now—what about the flight home?

> **s.d.** "one too many" or you can use a simpler phrase "too much work"
>
> **s.r.** "Three's Company"?
>
> **l.w.** Uh, "Friday"?
>
> **m.a.** according to translation book: Ménage à trois; but per fading memory of high school french: zoo for three.

080609

Peter Carlaftes has developed a new celebrity/reality show for America's Top Mediums called: *So You Think You Can Trance* . . .

> **m.p.** hilarious!!!!!
>
> **k.d.** LOL! =)
>
> **e.d.** i LOVE it.

080709

Peter Carlaftes figured out—that, all you gotta do is go to the nearest karaoke bar, grab the microphone and make puking noises—then sing the words *Nine Coronas* when the words *My Sharona* appears on the screen . . .

Guess who sang Karaoke the night before?

> **j.o.** Was it only nine?

080809

Peter Carlaftes just saw a German *a capella* oom-pah band called: *The Four Schnapps* . . .

One year on Facebook!!!!!!!!!

080909

Peter Carlaftes thinks, after hearing about *Jon and Kate Plus Eight*, their new post-divorce show should be called: *Breed 'em and Weep* . . .

> **e.d.** Perfection.

081009

Peter Carlaftes OK, OK . . . How about—since they're getting so old—Dead Rolling Stones Songs, like . . . *Hey, Hey, You, You Get Off A My Shroud* . . . (others?)

> **m.g.** how about wild hearses? ;)
>
> **p.c.** Love Wild Hearses . . . How about Wind Me Down?
>
> **d.w.** Exile on Slain Street?
>
> **p.c.** Waiting For A-Men?
>
> **d.w.** Play with Pyre?
>
> **m.g.** tee-hee.

081109

Peter Carlaftes wants to march against people with peace signs . . .

> **e.f.** I want to protest people who won't protest
>
> **r.s.** the peace sign originates from an upside-down hanged man. even saw that in "angels & demons"!
>
> **e.f.** how the hell does the upside down peace sign resemble a hanged man?
>
> **d.w.** You have never seen a hanged man, have you?

081209

Peter Carlaftes since the bum is playing the field, how about . . . *Jon and Kate Plus Date*? . . .

> **c.y.** no way he's yuckie!

081309

Peter Carlaftes is going to write a scathing exposé about the content children are forced to read in early education called: *Rhyme and Punishment* . . .

Dostoyevsky would punish me . . .

081509

Peter Carlaftes really wants to be Squeaky Fromme's Facebook friend . . . (could someone tell her, please?) . . .

> **a.s.** Done and done.
>
> **l.m.** Squeaky wants Peter to be Captain Hook when she does Peter Pan in dinner theater
>
> **s.i.** How long do you think it will be until her book deal is inked?
>
> **p.p.** i want to call her.
>
> **k.o.** I'll trade you for Manson's number. I know you have it.

081609

Peter Carlaftes was voted most likely to Exceed . . .

> **p.p.** the speed limit?

081709

Peter Carlaftes . . . Nobody knows . . . the Hubble I've seen: Carl Sagan (dying words) . . .

> **s.b.** That's going to lead to a new interjection, "Christ on the Hubble!"

081809

Peter Carlaftes just had the special shake at Malt Whitman . . . *Leaves of Wheatgrass!*

> **r.g.** Malt Whitman! LOL! that cracks muh butt!!
>
> **p.r.** Do they have Ezra Poundcake?
>
> **p.c.** yes . . . with robert frosting . . .
>
> **k.s.** Perhaps, Edgar Allen Pie?

081909

Peter Carlaftes thinks—Any pre-nup agreement should be—*The Declaration of Co-Dependence* . . .

Peter Carlaftes says . . . it's not easy doing nothing . . . you never know when you're finished . . .

> **m.f.** or when you really started

082009

Peter Carlaftes is on the brink of launching new website: *JFClay.Com* . . . so, if anyone wishes to assist in the recreation of the Kennedy Assassination in Claymation, my clay peeps'll talk with your clay peeps and—Hey! we'll let 'em go to lunch, like . . . it should be pretty cheap . . . they're made of clay, Right?

If anyone would like to help get this website up please have your head examined soon . . .

> **i.s.** You crack me up!

082109

Peter Carlaftes wonders—if . . . a secondhand job . . . is . . . really worth it?

> **v.l.** depends what the first hand job was like!
>
> **m.t.** sometimes.
>
> **l.h.** It is if you wait about two hours.
>
> **p.c.** now hold on here . . . i was thinking about buying a used car and you guys just turned it totally around here . . .
>
> **s.m.** good question
>
> **m.h.** yes it's worth it!
>
> **l.h.** Oh! I see . . . you're talking about getting a beater.

082209

Peter Carlaftes says, Woody Allen movies used to be much more Farrow-minded . . .

> **l.h.** And before that it was all about his Sex Keaton
>
> **p.c.** and before that they were of Lasser value . . .

Let l.h. get the "beater" of me on the previous entry —So . . .

082309

Peter Carlaftes wonders why Angelina Jolie keeps patting her chest—saying, *My Brad* . . . (?)

> **s.r.** Because she can

082409

Peter Carlaftes has an idea to reformat an old child's toy: A Jack-that-Thinks-Outside-of-the-Box . . . now, what should it look like?

> **r.l.** His head explodes.
>
> **p.c.** ok . . . function 1) it's head explodes. Next . . .
>
> **m.a.** The head pops OUT of the box when you wind it up?
>
> **m.d.** A shoe box with a human brain on top.
>
> **m.l.** Did you ever notice the people that liberally use the expression, "Think outside the box" are the people that are firmly ensconced inside of some box?
>
> **r.l.** Love m.d.'s idea. How about a tower of boxes with the largest at the base, growing smaller as it goes up (bread box, lunch box, shoe box, juice box . . .). Inside each box is a transparent head with a brain-dead brain. Then, our hero-brain pops out of the top box, lights up with neon colors—different colors for different sections of the brain, blinking off and on faster and faster (music too wouldn't hurt) until the brain explodes into glorious fireworks. I want one.
>
> **r.n.** Alec Baldwin.

082609

Peter Carlaftes certainly seems like they got the "Wealth" Care situation covered . . .

> **t.h.** That is about right. I think you may have something here.
>
> **e.f.** this ones a keeper
>
> **l.m.** are you really SOUPY SALES? You sound like him.

I'm fielding Soupy Sales offers . . . (as you read) . . .

Prior to publication, the great Soupy Sales passed away, RIP.

—Editor

082709

Peter Carlaftes is neither "near-" or "far-" sighted, rather . . . "hind-sighted" . . . (aren't we all) . . .

> **t.h.** You may need to get you some glasses for that condition.
>
> **p.c** yeah . . . some rose-colored ones, eh?
>
> **s.l.** Depends on whose hind you're sighting, I suppose.
>
> **a.c.** heart-shaped ones I say.
>
> **s.l.** In hindsight that sounds pretty good!

082809

Peter Carlaftes says—why not just put Ted Kennedy's picture on the trillion dollar bill?

> **g.w.** both sides

082909

Peter Carlaftes wouldn't back a Health Care Plan called: Sue Cross, Sue Shield . . .

> **m.d.** How 'bout "Single-payer Named Sue?"
>
> **p.c.** sounds like you'd be a little (johnny) cash-poor . . .

083009

Peter Carlaftes don't forget . . . at the opposite end of the spectrum there's *The Shirkaholic* . . .

> **l.h.** I'll respond to this one after my nap.
>
> **p.c.** at least you're not a hypoquit . . .

083109

Peter Carlaftes just got wind of the Swine Flu Conspiracy . . . Watch out! . . . They've put the Germ into Hand Sanitizers! . . . "It's People! It's People!" . . .

> **a.s.** lol. true.
>
> **s.l.** If enough people stop getting the inoculation, they'll put the germ in toothpaste. If they didn't create this hybrid flu then how do they explain human, pig and bird all mixed into one? Wait Jim Hensen, Miss Piggy and Big Bird must've had a three way after all!
>
> **p.c.** sesame streetwalkers? what's become of the world?

090109

Peter Carlaftes can't remember if Today is the "First" or "Worst" day of the rest of my Life . . .

r.f. First. First. Always the First.

m.g. if you're asking the question, I assume it's the "worst."

p.c. great . . . I'd much rather it be the worst, because . . . it'll be out of the way . . . unless, of course—it's also the last . . . and if it's also the last—then I—uhhh—argggghhhhh . . . (thump) . . . silence . . . sound of ambulance slowly rises . . . the end . . .

s.s. worst won't be the last, I tellya!

h.y. So true!

p.a. both?

k.t. the only one

090209

Peter Carlaftes can't seem to muster up any interest in the new Disney flick called: *Snow White and the Fantastic Four* . . .

> **l.h.** What if you called it . . . Snow White and the Fantastic Foursome?
>
> **p.c**. that would be a marvel . . .
>
> **d.l.** do you travel with a rimshot sound effect?? you should.
>
> **p.c.** wait . . . i want to see what the stretch man has from the fantastic foursome . . .
>
> **l.h.** of course . . . the fantastic fourskin!

090409

Peter Carlaftes is trying to tap into the failing retail market with a company that only accepts over-extended credit cards called: *Fears and NoBucks* . . .

> **l.h.** Perhaps they could merge with Nay See Penny . . .

l.h. and I are going to form new Vegas act: Punn and Duller . . .

090509

Peter Carlaftes . . . Number 1 reason for joining Facebook in the last year is: *Not-Working* . . .

> **s.s.** So true

090609

Peter Carlaftes what do Gore . . . Kerry . . . and McCain have in common? They are a Force to be "Second" with . . .

> **p.c.** and you can add the red sox to this list . . .
>
> **t.n.** 2nd? i'm predicting the sox won't even make the WC.
>
> **p.c.** is that the sign for european toilet (wc)?
>
> **l.h.** The Cubs have been in the WC for a hundred years.

090709

Peter Carlaftes . . . *over the EPA protected river and through the national park woods . . . to grandmother's foreclosed house we go . . .*

090809

Peter Carlaftes says, why can't we bring back the Cold War to fight the Swine Flu?

> **d.w.** That's an idea not to be sneezed at . . .

090909

Peter Carlaftes always leave 'em wanting more . . . (Sir Thomas More) . . . best quit while you're a-head . . .

[FINISH]

Order *Next Year on Facebook* right now.

[NEXT YEAR ON FACEBOOK]

[SNEAK PREVIEW]

Peter Carlaftes . . . jeez . . . the republicans have become so unpopular—that CBS is changing the name of that venerable game show to: *The Price is Left* . . .

BOOKS ON

Three Rooms Press

POETRY

by Peter Carlaftes
Drive By Brooding
I Canto Cantos
Nightclub Confidential
Progressive Shots
Sheer Bardom
The Bar Essentials

by Ryan Buynak
Enjoy the Regrets
Yo Quiero Mas Sangre

by Joie Cook
When Night Salutes the Dawn

by Kathi Georges
Bred for Distance
Punk Rock Journal
Slow Dance at 120 Beats a Minute

by Karen Hildebrand
One Foot Out the Door
Take a Shot at Love

by Dominique Lowell
Sit Yr Ass Down or You Ain't gettin no Burger King

by Jane Ormerod
Recreational Vehicles on Fire

by Susan Scutti
We Are Related

by Jackie Sheeler
to[o] long

by The Bass Player from Hand Job
Splitting Hairs

by Angelo Verga
Praise for What Remains

by George Wallace
Poppin' Johnny

PLAYS

by Madeline Artenberg & Karen Hildebrand
The Old In-and-Out

by Larry Myers
Mary Anderson's Encore
Twitter Theater

HUMOR

by Peter Carlaftes
A Year on Facebook

FICTION/MEMOIR

by Ronnie Norpel
Baseball Karma & The Constitution Blues

COMPILATION

by Peter Carlaftes
DrunkYard Dog (poems & plays)

Three Rooms Press *New York*
www.threeroomspress.com
info@threeroomspress.com

CPSIA information can be obtained at www.ICGtesting.com
Printed in the USA
LVOW08s1937031113

359782LV00002B/118/P